P9-CFJ-785

A Theological Approach to Art

A Theological Approach to Art

Roger Hazelton

Abingdon Press
NASHVILLE & NEW YORK

A THEOLOGICAL APPROACH TO ART

Library of Congress Catalog Card Number: 67-22165

SET UP, PRINTED, AND BOUND BY THE PARTHENON PRESS, AT NASHVILLE, TENNESSEE, UNITED STATES OF AMERICA

Preface

The interest of contemporary theology in the arts is not a new story. It has been frequently voiced in conferences, exhibitions, and a considerable body of writing on the subject. Why then should anyone want to draw attention again at this late date to themes and issues which have been explored so variously and thoroughly? I can only say that I believe a fresh and pertinent word is needed and should be attempted. As the dialogue between art and faith deepens, the contours of discussion change and new possibilities of mutual recognition emerge. That this is happening today cannot be doubted; it should be welcomed and given grateful theological expression.

Art, like Christian faith itself, is at home in the region of symbol—that realm in which meanings are not so much stated as they are evoked or illuminated, and in which events are not so much described as they are remembered and celebrated. This common zone is fertile, inexhaustible, and highly volatile; therein lie both its powers and its dangers. Yet it claims the effort and allegiance of us all, insofar as we are humanly capable of fashioning and responding to the world in which we live. Art and faith stand here on common ground, more common than the devotees of each ordinarily realize, and this ought to be pointed out and better understood.

More than this common ground, faith and art each need what the other has to give. Both are the poorer in the absence of such fruitful interchange of insights and materials. The long-continued estrangement, stretching back through most of the modern period, has atrophied the Christian imagination and has tended to trivialize, or at any rate to sterilize, much of the work in literature and the plastic arts especially. Not, of course, that there have been no genuinely great achievements based on the principles of "faith alone" or "art for art's sake." It was altogether right and necessary that artists should declare their independence of religious sanctions and that believers should be put on guard against idolatry or profanation of the holy in any form. But this is by no means to deny what ought to be affirmed—that when a way is open, when inhibitions and suspicions lose their force, faith and art can bring immense resource and support to each other. In Milton or Rouault, for example, what occurs is not a borrowing but a blending, a true marriage of elements drawn from a rich diversity of strength and significance. In instances like these, art and faith have found each other, and each has found itself in the other.

These things being so, and with the first exploratory efforts behind us, is the time not ripe for trying one's hand at a frankly theological interpretation of artistic endeavor? My own enthusiasm for such a risky task encourages, I suppose, what has to be called a certain boldness and impatience. Nothing so pretentious as a theological overview of all the arts is here in evidence.

I do, however, intend to show that there is indeed a Christian way of apprehending and appropriating works of art, not solely as documentation of the Christian reading of the human situation, but as "opening up a future" in which something like the older, almost forgotten harmonies between ways of making and ways of believing may perhaps be reestablished.

My hopes for those who read this slender book are of a piece with the reasons which have led me to write it. I wish that what contemporary artists in particular are doing and saying might be less of a foreign language than it is to those who call themselves Christians. I wish that those of us on the theological side of this deepening dialogue might know within ourselves and our work more of the "agony and ecstasy" which make art possible so that we would be less liable to raid the arts or use them for purposes of our own. Most earnestly, I hope that readers of this book may be helped to discover in the arts not only a profound mirroring of the human condition, but still more a *sursum corda,* a lifting up of the heart, a garment of praise to the Eternal.

* * *

It is a pleasure to record here my grateful indebtedness to Acadia University for the invitation to deliver the inaugural series of Hayward Lectures which, transcribed and expanded, form the structure of this volume. Especially I wish to thank Dean M. R. Cherry of the School of Theology for his generous and friendly welcome. Finally, I would express my appreciation to Mrs. Sue Taylor and Mrs. Judy Lyman for their valuable help with thc manuscript.

ROGER HAZELTON

Andover Newton Theological School
Newton Centre, Massachusetts

Contents

I *Art as Disclosure*

In this book we shall be engaged in the risky business of attempting to find the sort of meaning in works of art which answers to the expectations and urgencies of Christian faith. This enterprise is risky because the use of art for nonartistic purposes may, and often does, violate the integrity of the work of art itself. "We murder to dissect," as Wordsworth wrote. Much of the current discussion among theologians regarding the arts lies open to this danger, and to a quite discouraging degree. Yet if theologians did not attend at all to what is taking place in the contemporary arts, their understanding of man's being in the world would undoubtedly become even less pertinent to our needs and hopes than it now seems to be. So impressive a body of testimony to our true condition, so rich a texture of affirmations and negations regarding what being human means, can hardly be ignored or discounted by anyone who chooses in these days to speak up on behalf of Christian faith.

I

Moreover, if we wish to learn at firsthand something about the meaning of a work of art, we cannot always depend upon the artist himself to tell us what it is. Some artists become quite reticent, even secretive, when such questions of meaning are put to them by others. They prefer, as they insist, to let the work speak for itself. If it does not so speak, it must be counted as an artistic failure. And if it does, no further explanations or interpretations by the artist can add anything of significance to what has already been achieved. In a very real and noteworthy sense a poem, play, or painting simply is; it constitutes its own reason for being and requires no verbal propping up from the outside on the part of the artist or anybody else in order to do what it was designed to do.

Fortunately for theologians, however, there are other artists who tend to speak more freely and generously about the intentionality of their own work. Today especially, when so much in all the arts has the character of a radically new language, a strange new "firmament of symbol," we should be grateful for all the clues we can get. If it is agreed that any work of art is just that and not a kind of package which must be unwrapped in order that its meaning may be extricated, it is also plain that just by virtue of its existence or presence the artwork does raise questions of meaning and may even be said to demand that they be asked. There is another sense, equally valid with the first, in which what artists do is never finished, as their work only begins to live when they have brought it to creative completion. Then it calls us into something like a colloquy or running dialogue with itself in which we do not so much raid it for meanings of our own as discover its suggestive and evocative fertility as a meaning-stimulator. It is in this sense that "art is long, life is short." Knowing this, and rightly concerned to facilitate this sort of dialogue with their work, artists occasionally give tantalizing hints as to what they are about—hints which we cannot afford to disregard.

Pablo Picasso is one of these. In one of his rare moments of theorizing about his work he is reported to have ventured a definition of art itself. He said, "Art is a lie that makes us realize the truth." Like most apparent paradoxes this one teases and arrests the mind. What can it possibly be said to mean? How may truth, of all things, be realized by means of a deliberate invention or a carefully wrought illusion? And if it is actually truth that art is seeking, are there not better avenues to it than human imagination and its achievements can possibly provide? Picasso's remark is more than a playful aside or a provocative turn of phrase, perhaps intended only to upset temporarily our philistine composure vis-à-vis the artist's work. I believe Picasso is saying something of primary importance about the form and the intention of all art. Its form is that which is given to it by the human imagination, pliably responsive to the world of facts and events, selecting or magnifying this detail or that, shaping the raw stuff of the actual into fresh orderings of symbolic definiteness and potency. And art's intent is to declare just how things really are with us by devising a breakthrough which makes possible a sharing of experience without diminution or distortion. It was Georges Braque the painter who said, apropos of the charge that he made common things unrecognizable, "I don't have to distort; I'm only making something out of nothing."

This remark, like Picasso's, has a great deal to tell us concerning both the work of art and the artist's way of working. If, as the old saying has it, the purpose of art is to "hold a mirror up to nature," then it must be admitted that this is a very special kind of mirror, not a photographic plate. Whether we have in mind painting, novels, plays, poetry, or music, not to mention architecture or the dance, we are referring to art as a mediated immediacy, a contrived sincerity; in other words, as a lie that makes us realize the truth. This is exactly where our thinking about art as disclosure, as devising a breakthrough for the truth, must begin.

Take portraiture for example. At the turn of the century Auguste Rodin was working in Paris on his monumental tribute to the novelist Honoré de Balzac. Today in the main gallery of the Rodin Museum one may see well over a score of sketches and models made by the artist. When he finally brought his work to completion he left to the world an undoubted likeness of his subject. No one could mistake that massive figure for any other. There was accurate resemblance to the living human original in every line and surface of the statue. Yet what Rodin achieved was certainly no mere accuracy or verisimilitude. Without violating these canons he was able to go far beyond them. He conveyed a larger than life impression of the great novelist, one that was not less but more true than any collection of photographs could ever be. He did not set himself the impossible task of portraying Balzac as he was in his own lifetime, harried by responsibilities and cluttered up with relationships. He chose rather to let Balzac reveal himself through those very scenes of human life which he had described so candidly, attentively, uproariously in so many colors and contexts. Balzac by Rodin was more a world than a man, yet he was a man for all that. His image, as it was modeled in the statue with his name upon it, was more human than the man himself had been. Both in his own work and in Rodin's response to it, art was a lie—a lie that causes us to realize the truth.

Or take the theater. Here too we have to do with art as the realizing of truth through carefully wrought illusion. Was ever an actual man more wretched than King Lear, or a woman more desperately driven by conscience than Antigone? As I sit watching the play's action I may say to myself, "Yes, life's like that." To some degree I cease being merely an onlooker, a customer, and become caught up within the orbit of destiny which is presented to me. When characters like Antigone or Lear are brought upon the stage they not only report their own situations but reflect ours as well. By their imitation of human action, as Aristotle called it, the spectator is drawn with the actor into a milieu in which the inner meaning of all human action is released and stands forth for what it truly is. By consenting to this imitation, by agreeing to play this game according to dramatic traditions and conventions, we devise a breakthrough for the sharing of experienced truth. It is as if we could really understand our life only by stylizing it, letting truth speak its piece in a highly amplified voice under elaborately controlled conditions. In this same vein T. S. Eliot writes of the function of the theater as "imposing a credible order upon ordinary reality, and thereby eliciting some preception of an order in reality." Again, art is a kind of lie that makes us realize the truth.

Perhaps, in light of the examples that have been given, "lie" is too strong a word for what we have in mind. Picasso's definition does, however, direct our attention to the fact that only through images thrown up alongside the real can what is real come home to us, speak to us, take shape in us. The fashioning and using of symbols for the real is humanly necessary if the real is going to find its way to us in terms of truth —that is, of meaning about and for our life in the world. In saying this we have indicated both the process and the justification of the arts. This is also the vocation of the artist himself, as will be shown in the third chapter of this book. Artists work to devise symbolic breakthroughs by which hidden realities become manifest, even insinuating and evocative, as humanly realized truth.

Art, then, is disclosure. What is at stake in it is man's inveterate desire to shape the substance of his vision of the world for someone else to see. The artist—and he lives to some degree in each of us—wants at all costs to unmask whatever has become true for him, allowing or perhaps commissioning it to speak for itself to others as it has already spoken to him or is now in process of doing so. However, in order to bring about such a breakthrough of meaning the artist soon learns that it is necessary to disguise his vision, or at any rate to select and dwell upon one aspect of it until the part becomes in some way significant of the whole.

For the breakthrough must be devised; it is, if not a prevarication, at least a deliberate invention. A work of art is what Denis de Rougemont calls, most appropriately, a "trap for meditation." It must have within itself the power of attracting and then holding one's attention, of engaging the listener, reader, or spectator for at least a passing moment on its own terms, not his. In art a certain density is the very condition of transparency. Some symbols are better than others, but they are not on that account more ethereal or formless. A young and gravely smiling girl at a Dutch door, a dark and rounded sea-washed rock, or a man stopping by woods on a snowy evening, are all allurements and entrapments by which art catches us in its own net so that something of shareable, durable worth may be disclosed.

It is possible, of course, for both artists and their public to become so enamored of the trap-making process that the meditation which a work is aimed to encourage never quite occurs. Then technique takes the place of disclosure; in the absence of communicable value we are asked to admire virtuosity alone. "How did he do it?" Such a question, although always relevant, is secondary to another: "What is he trying to say?" Only when the latter question is asked has the work of art been successful in establishing the ground of meditative interchange between itself and its intended audience.

By "meditation" de Rougemont does not mean, I think,

the sort of prolonged dwelling upon an intellectual problem or period of mystical concentration with which this word is often confused. Art is productive of meditation in the sense that it demands that we pause, if for only an instant, in the press and rush of daily existence, and pause for the purpose that something may be given to us. It is, or ought to be, more a focus than a target, more a disclosure than a decorative embellishment. The greater the work of art, the more pronounced is this magnetizing quality.

Disclosure may mean discomfiture on the part of those for whom the "trap for meditation" is intended. Thus Ernst Barlach, the contemporary sculptor, explains his unusually arresting "confronting sculptures" as being "those that look at *you*." Here he is letting us in on a secret which has become almost proverbial with artists in our time. They try intentionally to put us on the spot before their work, not to display it for our mere approval. Of course, things being as they are, most artists have to sell their work if they are going to make art a vocation, and someone will need to be pleased by it. However, it has been demonstrated again and again that a public can be found whose sensibilities can be ruffled, if not violated, by works that apparently have the aim of taking us by force. To call a work "exciting" or "disturbing" is to give it a genuine measure of praise. Many contemporary artists stand ready to oblige.

One also thinks of Shakespeare's words in *Richard II:*

> Even through the hollow eyes of death
> I spy life peering; but I dare not say
> How near the tidings of our comfort is.

Here again is art taking the form of a disclosure of the unexpected and the paradoxical, making use of symbols not to tell us what we know already but to break through crusts of complacency and to shrink the distances which would otherwise keep the work of art from getting at us. If such art gives us pleasure—and it does—it is not the pleasure of agreement but of challenge and response, of being drawn into a "disclosure situation" where the usual defenses against our being really spoken to have been deftly and craftily removed by the artist.

II

Let us now attempt to be more precise about what is meant in calling art a manner and method of disclosure. Disclosure of what? We should be very wide of the mark indeed if we were to think of a work of art as a container or package with a "message" wrapped up inside. "Message art" is very seldom if ever genuine art. We do not have to abandon the search for meaning in art to recognize that it is not detachable or removable from the form in which it reaches us. When the "point" of a poem has been restated in another person's prose, the "point" has already been lost. A "Credo" composed by Mozart simply does not have the same translatable meaning as the creed repeated by a congregation, though the text is the same. In being set to music the creed has taken on another kind of life; it has entered a new and different order of meaning.

Religious art poses some especially acute problems in this connection. So much of it is so thoroughly insipid, trite, and cloying that it probably should not be termed art at all. When everything is geared for "getting the message" through pictorial instruction or musically induced emotion, should we be astonished if nothing happens either artistically or religiously? But happily there are exceptions, and they may be noted with gratitude. Van Gogh's painting of the Good Samaritan or Rembrandt's Jeremiah weeping over Jerusalem scarcely ever find their way into the churches; but they belong there, for they convey the very qualities of faith which are sadly lacking in most of what is presented in churches for our pious edification. The purpose of art is not to inform or instruct, but to disclose; and this is more, not less, true of the arts of the church.

What of art as the instrument of propaganda? Anyone who traveled in Nazi Germany will recall the made-to-order quality of much of the music, novels, and painting of those unhappy days. The shrill marches, the dreary processions of storm troopers or Hitler youth, the stories of undeviating obedience overriding all ties of family or friendship—one would certainly be wary of calling this any kind of art. What it was, of course, was simple propaganda, miscalled at the time "art with a national purpose." It asked nothing but to be agreed with and emulated.

Yet this negative judgment on so-called "message art" in propaganda form should not be misunderstood. It does not mean that discussion of current public issues is forbidden the artist; not at all. John Milton wrote tracts for the times—embittered, partisan, impassioned—without breaking the spell or going against the grain of great literature. Goya in his time made an indelible record of the shooting of defenseless peasants, mixing his palette with a kind of holy anger. In our own century Picasso's "Guernica" takes sides in the Spanish civil war, portraying the utter helplessness of people and animals subjected to saturation bombing, yet also their outrage at what is happening to them. No one hesitates to call these works genuine and deeply moving art, not in spite of the occasions or provocations that inspired the artists, but because of them.

Yet here again there is no message to be extracted from these works; whatever meaning is disclosed is given in and with the works themselves, not as an ingredient to be factored out, but as a total impact claiming our involvement, bringing home our stake in this and every human struggle. It is rather foolish to inquire whether this meaning might not be otherwise or better stated, for then it would not be *this* meaning but some other which had been read into what is given for our seeing.

We are not to suppose, then, that art is the disclosure of something pre-artistic or nonartistic; it is not a package waiting to be unwrapped in order that a shining "truth" may be discovered inside. However, may not something positive be said about what is disclosed in works of art? More especially, are there not conditions which may be met by those who would "realize the truth" conveyed in art?

Attention is the first requirement, naturally. This requirement is as difficult as it is also self-evident. By attention is meant listening until we really hear, looking until we really see—de Rougemont's "meditation" again. Surely we owe every serious artist at least that much or we can scarcely blame him for not "reaching" us.

What is still sometimes termed "art appreciation" begins with a state of exposure to a given work, then deepens into an effort of attention more or less deliberate and sustained. Such effort does not come naturally to very many of us. We are mostly tourists in our dealings with the arts. That is, we come and go, more interested in obvious quick benefits or in forming right opinions than in letting the artwork grow upon us, move toward us out of its own depth. If there is to be any real conveying of meaning in such experiences, however, the aperture of our sensibilities must be held open long enough for genuine exposure to take place. Attentiveness on our part is the price of admission to realizing aesthetic truth.

It can be laid down as a pretty reliable rule that while artists usually mean what they say, they do not always say exactly what they mean. They may be playing with us only to keep our interest or leading us down enticing bypaths for the sake of a later rendezvous. An authentic work of art has both a surface and a depth, and the relation between them may not be a matter of direct progression at all, but a broken line of indirect suggestion. The canvases of Juan Miro, for example, are painted, we are told, in a "language . . . secret, ambiguous, and above all poetic." His interpreter goes on to say:

A biting irony is present in his work. . . . Miro's moods are sombre by nature. Everything in his world is wrong! Is there not a strange distance between this star and that woman? It is too close not to be threatening. Does not this woman running on her head in space leave in her wake a menacing phosphorescent trail? Miro is one of the painters who best know how to translate the anguish of night, where suddenly apparitions appear in the desertlike countryside, beneath the metallic light of the moon. These beings dismembered under the blows of hostile forces, which tear them asunder, attempt to join up without ever completely succeeding. . . . The struggle against death and degradation never ceases to be moving and poetic. The frontiers between life and death are not definite.[1]

An estimate such as this is clearly the result of careful, prolonged attention to Miro's works, and it also gives evidence of willingness on the part of the beholder-interpreter to be taken by surprise by what at first seem drolleries or fantasies, but which turn out on closer inspection to be speaking truth of a higher magnitude.

If in art we do not always find said what is meant, we usually find meant what is said. Indeed, taken as a

[1] Guy Weelen, *Miro 1940-1955* (New York: Tudor, n.d.), pp. 1-4.

group, contemporary artists are notably ready to risk public disapproval, censure, or misunderstanding in order to remain faithful to their own hard-won convictions. Often the more unpopular these are, the better. Like Miro, the artist in our time is regularly found on the side of the humane; even his depictions of brokenness or estrangement constitute a courageous protest against everything that dehumanizes man. He may or may not join causes and sign manifestos, yet his very effort to express the lineaments of dislocation and reversal is a kind of prophetic refusal to acquiesce to what he regards as the dominating forces of the age. An admirable seriousness and moral integrity underlie his work. He is a man who means what he says.

Not that the serious artist is trying to get at us through his work for purposes ulterior—or perhaps anterior—to the creative imagination itself. One may suspect that this is taking place, for instance, in the writing of James Baldwin today; but such a charge would be unfair, at least as an overall criticism, because Baldwin can and does sheathe moral indignation and icy contempt in a style that is amazingly pliant and alive. One does not have, except at rare intervals, the impression that a social reformer is using literature to advance a worthy cause. What we have is artistic work of social significance, as we were wont to say several decades ago; but is there any good reason why racial injustice should not become occasion and material for compelling disclosure in the arts? To put it a bit differently, is not injustice among men in some real way a failure of the human imagination? And is not the arousal and repair of the imaginative faculty in man precisely what art seeks to bring about?

We should probably not be put off the track too easily by those artists who declare firmly that their work must simply be judged on its own artistic merits and needs to be viewed only in aesthetic perspective in order to be understood. They can scarcely be blamed for this, as they have so often been raided for meanings foreign to or even incompatible with their own creative enterprise. They have rightly been unwilling to allow their works to be turned into something else by outsiders who find only what they expect to find. Suffering from this misuse, they sometimes become drawn into a deliberate isolation from the wider community of meanings shared in common experience. They may then turn to technical experimentation, to sharpening tools and skills, and may even take pride in becoming unintelligible or esoteric in their work. This is a contemporary version of the old maxim, "art for art's sake," which has often in the past served as artistic self-protection and self-justification in the face of public disapproval or indifference. Yet even this turning in of art upon itself may help to remind us that "otherness in reality," to use H. D. Lewis' term, is exactly what artists work to bring to our awareness.

There is undoubtedly a kind of paradox involved in speaking of art as disclosure. On the one hand, it is plainly true that art seeks to establish a world of its own and to invite us into that world. Arthur Miller, commenting upon his recent play *After the Fall,* asserted that the play was not *about* something, but hopefully *was* something. An artist is a maker who wants what he has made to stand by itself. But on the other hand, art that deserves to be called great possesses a strange capacity to lead us beyond its presented surface toward quickened awareness, perhaps even rediscovery, of the common surrounding world that is both wider and deeper than art's own. So Arthur Miller, having seemed to say the very opposite, then went on to remark that what his play was about was "the terrifying fact of human choice." Both statements should be taken seriously, as each throws needed light on the other.

What truth does art make us realize? Picasso's tantalizing sentence does not at all suggest that truth in art is of a single or simple kind. On the contrary, the way is left quite open for a rich complexity and fecundity of human meaning, which is as it should be. Art's substance is as many-faceted, as confusingly diverse, as the texture of human experience itself. And yet throughout, as Nathan Scott has said well, "The greatest and most vital art . . . wants, as it were, to make all things new, in order that we might marvel at the sheer thereness of them, at the fact that they exist in one way rather than in a thousand other possible ways." [2] In other words, art is intent on making possible a seeing of things as they are —for instance, "imaginary gardens with real toads in them"—an enterprise that has something singular and urgent to do with realizing truth.

This is relatively easy to grasp in cases where a given human condition is presented for our seeing. The satirical drawings of Hogarth or Daumier come readily to mind as evidence. Forlorn chimney sweeps or ridiculously pompous lawyers captured in unerring lines are drawn from life, yet also have a new life conferred upon them. Such artists want to show us how it was, but with the strong conviction that it should have been otherwise. Such implicit protests against the distortion or degradation of the human image have both aesthetic and moral justification, as do the somber, stirring drawings of Käthe Kollwitz in our own time. They make us realize the truth that human misery is itself an unforgettable sign of human dignity.

[2] In "Faith and Art in a World Awry," *The Student World,* No. 2 (1962), p. 203.

The case is somewhat different with those works of art in which irony or pathos are not so prominent a creative force. An artist may wish simply to make us see a familiar object or routine event afresh, as if it had never been seen before. Van Gogh did this supremely with his paintings of landscapes and interiors. He looked at fields of grain until he saw them blazoned with fire from the sun. He could paint a pair of old shoes as the very symbol of human toil and care so evocatively that a small boy with his parents in a museum on a Sunday afternoon would stop and ask, "Mother, whose shoes are those?" Here the truth art makes us realize is that which has been called the "shock of recognition" or "effective surprise."

Obviously this is not the sort of truth that can be stated in just so many words. It resists translation into other languages than that of art itself. It cannot be reduced to mere emotional impact; all emotionalistic theories of art, as Nathan Scott has shown, fail just at the point where they succeed, in dissolving the aesthetic experience into something else—psychology for instance. But neither can truth in art be rendered adequately in purely intellectual categories; for although what Paul Tillich called "the shock of being" is undeniably involved, artistic truth does not submit to generalized abstractions about being-as-such. Being has its residence in actuality, in the given "thinginess" of the real world; and if things may become, as in the arts, true windows looking out upon being, it is nonetheless to be remembered that such windows are indispensable for human seeing. They frame a perspective, afford a vantage point which would otherwise be impossible for us. A work of art may cause us to encounter truth in the form of compassionate identification, as so often in Rembrandt, or in that of brutal exposure, as in the plays of Tennessee Williams. Either way, what matters is that an artist's seeing of the way things really are should awaken in us a new power of seeing not only these but other things as well.

III

To whom is art disclosure? That is, do artists actually want company, and do they intend to communicate truth to us? This is a fair question because we are so often told that artists have no such desire, that they do their work in a "take it or leave it" manner and couldn't care less whether the rest of us are moved by it or not. I recall a sculptor-in-residence at a western college who used to take this line with his students. He would declare that he did his work for no one but himself and did not care whether it was noticed by others. The strange fact was, however, that his sculptures were all huge assemblages of several kinds of material, obsessed with the distortion and erosion of the human figure. They would never find their way into someone's living room, but they were very clearly made to be noticed, reacted to, and not ignored. This sculptor's work spoke far more loudly than the things he said about it, and made what he said at least dubious if not questionable.

The intent of all art is to communicate, whether this is admitted or not. This may not be an artist's primary purpose at the moment, but it is an ultimate or penultimate one all the same. And if the artist asserts that he does not want to communicate, this is one of the ways in which he is communicating and we had better listen when he says it.

Yet there are genuine problems with this much-abused word, "communication," as a means of making clear the forms and impulses of artistic disclosure. For many today communication is regarded and employed as a kind of egocentric violence; it means getting across my message to you, forcing it upon you in order to make you hear it. Hence I become preoccupied with questions like, "Do you read me? Am I coming through to you? Do you get what I mean?" Communication then is supposed to have occurred when this effort to impose my meaning upon you has been successful. Hence too the vast proliferation of techniques of communication, on the theory that the more people reached, and the more quickly and directly, the better. In our time, it is sadly true, communication tends to be understood as "public relations" even in the most private sectors of our experience; it usually has something to do with selling a product, even if that product should be myself or my vision of the world.

Now there can be little question that if this is what communication means, the arts are generally not much interested in it. To be sure, some artists allow their work to be used for commercial purposes through the mass media; but one suspects that it is largely because they "have to live" rather than because they see this as intrinsic to their vocation. It must also be admitted that compulsiveness in the creative process is not to be disregarded; there are artists who, like Nietzsche, have to say: "I write to get rid of my thoughts, because I must." We cannot deal at this point with the involuntary, ecstatic dimension of the artist's way of working or with the explosive character of some of his achievements. It will perhaps be enough to point out that all art does not readily fit into the categories of expressionism and that all communicativeness of which artists are capable is not of the anxious, self-concerned type.

Possibly "dialogue" is a more accurate term than "communication" for getting at this view of art as disclosure to another. Sir Herbert Read, whose knowledge and judgment in these matters should be highly valued, says that all art has a dialogic, dialectical character. Art is not only a making, but a showing-forth which claims some sort of response.

Response can neither be guaranteed nor controlled by any built-in artistic devices. When all is said and done, the confrontation with a work of art is personal, hidden, finally free; it does not come about as the result of an engineering job. If some kind of interior dialogue does take place, it will not be the explainable product of prearranged factors, but rather "deep calling unto deep." The point, however, is that in art we have unmistakable tokens that such a calling and responding do occur and are intended. Nietzsche's thoughts, once they are off his chest, become philosophy and literature for all the world to argue about and ponder. Even when we feel that we are being let in on a secret almost unbearably intimate, the fact is that the secret has been consciously and artfully shared with us.

There is both loss and gain in this dialogic process of disclosure in the arts. There is loss of intensity and immediacy in the original creative situation which launched the work into being; once the story has been told, the picture painted, or the music composed, the artist's ardor has cooled, his energies have been channeled. But there is also gain: in "bringing words to heel" or "making something out of nothing" the artist has been able to bring his private vision up to the threshold of another's consciousness and so to open a communicable future with that other.

In the performing arts, of course, this communicative function comes through most clearly. Here the vocal or instrumental interpretation of a work of art is itself art; neither would be conceivable or possible without the other. A Bach toccata and fugue played on a baroque organ by Albert Schweitzer or by a full symphony orchestra—one may seriously ask whether they are performances of the same work, except in a musicological sense. Even if "the play's the thing," what real harmony exists between Sir Henry Irving's Hamlet and Sir John Gielgud's except the lines that each must learn and speak? The performing arts make obvious something that holds for all the arts—that although communicable and communicated, truth in art is not a commodity which changes hands nor some kind of essence to be extracted and distributed.

Does the reproduction of works of art inhibit or facilitate communicable disclosure? The question is pertinent in an age which knows art chiefly through mass-produced copies, recordings, or editions. That public exposure to the arts is thereby greatly increased is obvious, but can this be properly termed genuine encounter with the kind of truth which art wishes us to realize? Does mass reproduction constitute a hindrance rather than a help? Just how "live" is an album of a Beethoven piano sonata which has been produced by cutting and splicing several tapes of a single performer's work, engineered with an eye to maximum stereophonic accuracy and flawless technical finish? How much of musical performance is dependent for its aesthetic worth upon the visual presence of the performer? It would seem that reproduction by mechanical means, however technically effective, is a sword that cuts both ways: it undoubtedly makes possible a greater degree of concentration on the listener's part, yet it also leaves him without the corporate and visible experience which the work was originally designed to bring about. Should it therefore be surprising if a listener pays closer attention to the surface of the sound than to the depth of the music?

Some years ago an American publisher brought out a massive edition of Tolstoy's *War and Peace,* a handsome volume complete with charts, maps, and a long introduction by Clifton Fadiman. Reviewing the book, Christopher Morley commented that only one thing was lacking. Between the introduction and the text of Tolstoy's novel, he said, there should have been inserted a page with these words written on it: "From here on,

Leo, you are on your own." With all the good intentions in the world, do we not often simply make impossible the very confrontation looking toward disclosure which mass-reproduced art presumably seeks to establish? I say presumably, as this is very far from being clear.

To members of a generation to which works of art are known primarily through reproduction, confrontation with an original may come with something of a shock. This may or may not be the shock of recognition, but in most instances it leaves one permanently dissatisfied with lesser substitutes, even if these are more "perfect" in some technical sense. I had seen reproductions of Rouault's painting called "The Holy Face" for many years before I came upon the original in the Musée d'Art Moderne in Paris—the colors were dimmer, the size smaller than I had expected—but then I knew that no reproduction could ever do it justice. Why? Not because of the greater "beauty" of the original, whatever that might mean, but because of its very roughness of texture, abruptness of line, and suggestions of depth beneath the plastic surface. Those dark, staring eyes, making with the long nose the sign of the cross within the face, were looking at *me*. And I had never before realized the regal, ruby-like quality of the bloody splotches that frame the livid greenish background; now they began to disclose victory in and through the desperation of defeat. No reproduction had been able to conjure up such depth of seeing before, and thereafter it would only be able to echo and confirm it.

There is a statement made by Ananda Coomaraswamy which is very much to the point when we are thinking of art as the experience of dialogic disclosure: "The artist is not a special kind of man, but every man is a special kind of artist." This surely means that a basis for a community of meaning, of truth, exists already in our common humanity—in this case a community of *homo faber,* man the maker of images and fashioner of symbols. Far too much aesthetic theory has been predicated on the mistaken notion that here we are dealing with a subject-object relation analogous to visual cognition, so that aesthetics is at bottom a branch of epistemology. Thus the very foundation of a shared and shareable truth at the fully human level is analyzed away.

But this will not do at all. The fact is, art is a human enterprise involving and indeed requiring the uniquely intellectual, moral, and spiritual capacities. Art belongs indubitably to that shaping, form-giving activity, bent on achieving order and worthful meaning, which we know as culture. It is therefore personal and interpersonal in both the vision that is shared and the motivation that stirs that vision into being. It exists to be seen, heard, read, responded to by others who are also special kinds of artists, whose ability to make response is their native human endowment and experience. If in the community of the arts there should be, as is presently the case, a small but exceedingly vocal group whose members believe that the prevailing culture has nothing to offer them and are self-consciously set apart from and against it, nevertheless even this disengagement may be for our common good and we must be instructed by it.

In a Christian context we may be encouraged to speak of the ministry of the arts. An artist himself may not see his work in this perspective, to be sure. Yet we Christians ought to be prepared for the fact that authentic forms of ministry seldom if ever announce themselves as such. We should also readily admit that means of grace are not restricted to churchly channels in the world which God has made and acted to redeem. The ministry performed by the arts is not less real because it is disavowed or concealed. Indeed it may be all the more effective and significant on that account. It is no mean ministry to take the raw stuff of life—vast, elusive, often discordant—and then so reshape it that its inner texture of grace and glory, shallowness or brutishness, is disclosed. Paul Klee, whose work is justly admired in theological circles today, put into memorable words this unique ministry of disclosure. "Real art," he said, "plays an unknowing game with ultimate things—and yet achieves them!"

Exactly so; and whether by playful indirection or by prophetic dedication, art therefore ministers the mystery of the real to us.

IV

Such a seeing and offering up of life as the arts achieve deserve to be understood and valued in the light of Christian faith. Were we to speak of art as human revelation we would not be far from the truth of the matter. There have been many ways of teaching the meaning of revelation in our theological traditions, not all of which are equally useful for the present purpose. For instance, it does not help to illumine the disclosing function of art if we conceive revelation as the handing down of moral commands from on high; artists do not presume to be, nor should they be confused with, authoritative spokesmen for a divine imperative. Neither can we get much benefit from the notion that there are "revealed truths," since here again the supposition of a one-way communication giving information in propositional form is totally incongruous with what transpires in the arts. The point of capital importance is that these renderings of what revelation means are as inadequate for theological as much as for aesthetic understanding. There must be some better clue than either of these for doing what we have in mind.

And such a clue exists; in fact the dominant theological trends of the recent past in Western Christianity have been largely devoted to discovering and using it. Revelation (*apokalypsis*, "unveiling") has in one way or another been the chief concern of theologians such as Barth and Brunner. They have been joined by many others in a massive effort to speak of revelation as God's own speaking to man in living confrontation through actual historical events both past and present, thereby eliciting the free response of human faith.

In this interpretation the word "response" has fundamental import, so much so that this word has almost become axiomatic and unquestioned as conveying the central meaning of faith. As response, faith is receptive but not passive; it is not, strictly speaking, a human power but a gift of God. "Response" points emphatically to the priority and initiative of God himself in his revelation, which as Hans Frei characterizes it, is *"the* I-Thou encounter *par excellence*." [3] Revelation consists not of truths about God or even of truth from God, but of the dynamic self-disclosure of God himself to human selves. As Revealer, God is the eternally active "I" who

[3] "Religion: Natural and Revealed," in *A Handbook of Christian Theology*, Marvin Halverson and Arthur A. Cohen, eds. (Cleveland World, 1958), p. 315.

addresses man as "thou" and makes man capable of hearing and doing the divine will.

All this and much more like it is, as I say, axiomatic in recent theology, as exemplified in the work of men such as Brunner, who speaks of "truth as encounter," and Barth, for whom revelation means that God remains the Subject (and not the "object" of man's faith) even when we think and talk about God in the light of revelation.

Now how can this understanding help in relation to the arts? It clearly refers solely to God, only indirectly and consequently to human experiences. And yet its models are all drawn from personal and interpersonal relationships; the "word-event" of Christ is spoken, or occurs, within the tangled web of earthly circumstance and worldly culture; and far from displacing or canceling the human, God's self-disclosure in Christ is the very taking up and consecrating of the human.

Let us then try to think of art as a kind of human analogue to revelation, with full realization of the risks and limitations involved. We shall not be saying that man can do what only God can do, but we shall perhaps discover how the work of man stands forth when illumined by the word of God. For if man himself may be said in the Christian perspective to be a work of art—that is, made in the image of God—then may not man's own works be said to shine in reflected light? In Berdyaev's arresting phrase, our history is "the reciprocal revelation of man in God."

It must freely be admitted, in the first place, that this Christian way of thinking about human life and work seems diametrically opposed to that which gets expressed in contemporary art, at least in large sectors of it. What does his art know or tell of man being open upward to God, reflecting "as in a mirror the splendor of the Lord," a creature, but an image of the transcendent? Do we not rather have man pictured as "full of holes and gaps, faceless, riddled with doubts and negations, starkly finite"? [4] Taking a random sampling, one would certainly be obliged to say that anything like a Christian vision of the human is conspicuously lacking. The difference is not that between an optimistic and a pessimistic view, but goes much deeper. It is simply the difference, in the words of Pascal, between the misery of man without God and the greatness of man with God.

But in the second place, we Christians cannot rightly expect modern artists to achieve the impossible. They can only give us what they see, and there are many valid reasons why they do not see, generally speaking, with the eyes of faith. Do not our own theologians, in-

[4] William Barrett, *Irrational Man* (New York: Doubleday, 1958), p. 54.

tent upon salvaging "the rumor that there is a God," find it painfully necessary to reflect upon God's "eclipse," "absence," or even "death"? This deprivation of God is surely a common feature of our life today, and it would be inconceivable if artists had not detected and described it. That they actually have done so, while it makes Christian conversation with the arts undoubtedly difficult, makes such conversation both imperative and highly opportune. Do we not all alike live in a secular, "desacralized" world, and may not a radically godless art become a kind of negative witness to the God whom we have all forgotten, most of all in our religiousness?

Thirdly, works of art have Christian meaning to a Christian believer; whoever created them and whatever their ostensible themes, they are potentially revelatory to him who sees and hears according to Christ. For it is our faith that "in him, and through him, and to him are all things,"—in short, the whole world has been given its true meaning by God's deed in Jesus. Hence Christians have no reason to view the secular and profane things of this world with either superiority or suspicion. Granted the "special revelation" which God has given us of himself in Christ, should we not be attentive to the "general revelation" whereby all things are coherent with the one thing needful? Otherwise what does the lordship of Christ, wrested from dark, demonic powers for man's everlasting good, really mean to us?

Yes, there is a way in which the arts of our contemporary culture may be viewed and valued by those of us whose first encounter with them appears utterly negative or hostile. This was suggested to me in a conversation with a distinguished German poet, Rudolf-Alexander Schroeder. We were talking about whether Shakespeare and Homer could properly be called Christian poets and what such a name could add to or take away from their work. Then Dr. Schroeder said, "All this reminds me of the parable of the water that was made wine. When as a Christian I read Homer or Shakespeare, the water in their work becomes wine." Not that my faith confers a revealing value which works of art would not possess otherwise, but that my faith in the divine generosity disclosed in Christ encourages me to go deeper, returning to the work again and again if need be, in order that I may be nourished and gladdened thereby.

Finally, art as human revelation is most indubitably gracious in effect precisely when it dwells upon what is broken, tormented, emptied of meaning in our actual world. We who find God's love revealed centrally in Christ should know something about dereliction and crucifixion, lostness and estrangement. Might we not therefore be expected to respond to the contemporary artist's report of these things with a shock of recognition and identification? Indeed, we cannot see the truth which harbors at the heart of Christian faith without responding in this way. There was a clown in Munich, very popular with the circus-going public, who used to have a familiar routine. He would come onto the stage, all dark except for a beam of light in the center, in which the clown went round and round frantically looking for something. A policeman entered from the wings and asked, "What have you lost?" The clown answered, "The key to my house." After helping him search for a while the policeman said, "Are you sure you lost it here?" "No, over there," the clown replied, pointing toward the darkness. "Then why on earth are you looking for it here?" The answer: "Because there's no light over there."

Is there a better image for the state of man and the world than is reported in the arts of our time? The search for something that has been lost, the useless key that isn't there, the darkness of the absurd, the pathos of being human—all is caught up and enacted so that we too may be grasped by it. This is human revelation which strikes home with particularly poignant force to the Christian, who thinks he knows where the key is but may be quite unaware that he too has lost it.

II Art as Embodiment

Theologians often have the awkward experience of meeting friendly old words in strange new disguises. "Creation" is surely one of these. Within the religious vocabulary it has a place of time-honored importance, signifying of course the art by which God brought the world into being. But today, having been borrowed and drained of its Christian content, creation may apply to anything from a new dress to a chef's salad. The word "creative" is probably employed most frequently in advertising offices as a term of approval meaning what is strikingly novel or original. It becomes easy to forget that once it had something to do with God.

Also in the realm of the arts we are accustomed to hearing of the creative process, or of the artist's work as a creation. In this usage we hark back to the Romantic period, when these words gained currency in art criticism and aesthetics. Then they still had something to do with inspiration, whatever that might mean, although any reference to God that may have been intended was already more polite than theologically earnest. My intention in this chapter is to show that these words are indeed illuminating when applied to art and artists, but that they should be taken in their classical theological sense. Or, to put the matter just a bit differently, we shall be venturing to understand artistic creativeness in the reflected light of the Christian doctrine of creation. Such a task of thought may not prove to be easy; it has often been suggested but seldom actually attempted in recent theological discussion; and the way is clearly open in the deepening dialogue of faith with art to take this proposal with the seriousness it deserves.

I

In order for this to happen, some old metaphysical dragons need slaying and some old dogmatic slumbers must be broken. Chief among the first is the inveterate scholastic prejudice that understands creation rather rigidly as *ex nihilo,* out of nothing, meaning absolute metaphysical zero. And in the second group there is the well-worn theological assertion that creation establishes an infinite distance between God and his world of creatures, such that no human thought or effort can of itself begin to bridge the great gulf God has fixed in the very nature of things.

Ex nihilo is an essentially philosophical elaboration of the biblical saga of the world's beginning, designed to protect the radically miraculous and supernatural character of God's creative act and to put an end to what would otherwise be an unending regress of cause and effect. Insofar as this term *creatio ex nihilo* underscores the scriptural and Christian truth that the world owes its existence ultimately to a transcendent Will and not to a cosmic craftsman or Platonic demiurge, it fills a useful function. But if it goes beyond this, as it appears to do, declaring that creation is utterly different from any natural event or human act we know, that "nothing" must be paradoxically assumed before there can be a world at all, then *creatio ex nihilo* raises more theological questions than it answers.

It is interesting that St. Augustine preferred to speak of creation *de nihilo,* from nothing, possibly because he kept his thinking closer to the Bible. When we read the Genesis accounts, especially that given in the second chapter, we must agree with Gerhard von Rad that the narrative "moves not so much between poles of nothingness and creation as between the poles of chaos and cosmos." [1] This is because in Genesis the accent falls so heavily upon God's action in creation rather than upon his absoluteness or self-containment of being. Creation does not happen all at once, nor is it entirely one complete and single act; God calls, forms, distinguishes, and names the multifariousness of the world. Indeed, the more carefully we read and ponder the story told in Genesis, the more creation seems to take on the characteristics of a work of art.

The dogmatic assertion that creation fixes man in finitude and keeps him at his properly creaturely distance from the Creator is also due for some surprises when it is placed in confrontation with the Bible. As soon as man is created, he is called by God to take part

[1] In *Genesis, A Commentary* (Philadelphia: Westminster, 1961), p. 80.

in the ongoing creation. His work is twofold: he is given the power and right of naming the animals and of taming them. This is surely to say that man himself is to be God's helper in creation. Upon him is conferred "dominion over the fish of the sea and the birds of the air"; he is permitted, nay commanded, to fashion his own relationships and find his own meanings within the world in which God has given him a creative place and function. Creation, therefore, cannot be rightly understood without due recognition of man's deputyship or partnership with God in bringing the world into being. Again, in reading the Bible we become awakened to the truth that in the firm words of Karl Barth: "By the grace of God man is not nothing. He is God's man. . . . We cannot say and demand and expect too much or too great things from man."[2]

The Christian doctrine of creation therefore yields a truly magnificent and ennobling view of man, particularly in his cultural activities. Of course there is something else to be said too, and other doctrines such as those of the Fall and of Redemption spell out man's estrangement from God and his need of a mediator and savior sent by God. Yet insofar as man is created in the

[2] Quoted by Harvey Cox in *The Secular City* (New York: Macmillan, 1965), p. 83.

very likeness of the Creator, and in spite of his mishandling and abuse of that likeness, he is "God's man," and this is his essential nature which points toward his true destiny. The doctrine of creation is not a theory of how the world began, a Christian substitute for the sciences of astronomy and geology. Rather, it is our way of understanding whatever is human and natural in the clear light of faith that to be a creature means to participate in the intention and action of the Creator.

Turning again to the consideration of human art, must we not find in it at least a simile or image of divine creativeness? We do not have to go so far as Robert Browning, who compared the artist to God and in his poem "Abt Vogler" claimed that the musician in particular overcomes the laws of nature and even is freed from human limitations in his creative work. Yet the likeness between human and divine creation continues to thrust itself upon our attention and demands some sort of Christian understanding.

Denis de Rougemont prefers to speak of art as "composition" rather than "creation," feeling that the former is the more modest and Christian term. Thus understood, the work of art is more a new arrangement of materials already at hand than it is a bringing into being through cooperation with God's gracious power. If we hesitate to follow de Rougemont in this narrowing and tightening of the meaning of the work of art, as I think we should, it is because both Christian and aesthetic considerations suggest a more generous view. Do not Shakespeare's words about the poet have a more ample, accurate ring of truth? "Imagination bodies forth the forms of things unknown" and "gives to airy nothing a local habitation and a name." Do we not have here a firsthand, authentic clue to the creative process evidenced in the arts which would be disastrous to neglect?

So to think of art as a bodying-forth, an embodiment, means that the analogy with divine creation is more seriously taken and carried through. It may have been that this was what Friedrich Schlegel had in mind in laying down his principle that all art was religious. If we are to accept this principle, it will be useful to recall as well Tillich's well-known distinction between what is explicitly and implicitly religious in a work of art. Not all art is consciously or ostensibly religious in either motive or meaning; but all art can be said to disclose, directly or deviously or surreptitiously, that "ultimate concern" which is the signature of the religious.

But whether or not it is important to call all art religious in this twofold sense, the point is that a religious understanding of the artistic enterprise is really open to us. The work of giving "to airy nothing a local habitation and a name," when all is said and done, remains mysterious. Just how and why and what the artist creates is finally the sort of question that forbids complete explanation in psychological or philosophical terms, however much light these may cast upon it. Must there not be some continuity, some common denominator of meaning, between what man does in the arts and what God does in creation?

Nicolas Berdyaev, the Russian Orthodox lay theologian whose book on Dostoevsky is still the very best, had much to say on this whole subject. He interpreted the creation of man in God's own image to mean that man thereby became a creator too, called to free spontoneous activity in fulfillment of his Creator's inmost will. Art, wrote Berdyaev, is a creative breakthrough into a transfigured world, and its meaning "lies in the fact that it is the anticipation of the transfiguration of the world." [3]

Does Berdyaev's thesis seem too glowing and unrealistic? Analytical psychologists have suggested quite another view. Artistic creativeness is regarded as the expression of the unconscious in which compensation and sublimation play their prominent role. Thus warmth of color in Matisse or the line of a theme of Mozart are to be elucidated as originating in the artist's unconscious but assuming the conscious form of wish fulfillment,

[3] In *Slavery and Freedom* (New York: Scribner's, 1944), p. 241.

defense mechanism, striving for recognition, or some other psychological effect. These analyses are fascinating and have undeniable force, especially when artists tend to be neurotically burdened with conflicts and tensions of which their work is in some degree the resolution. Clinical evidence abounds in support of this psychological view.

However, the real question is whether this is the last word to be said on the subject. Most assuredly it cannot be. Why should not struggle and suffering in a man or woman of heightened sensitivity become productive of clearer seeing, creative of new forms of meaning? Aesthetic truth and value do not disappear simply because their psychological conditioning can be investigated and described. We still have art as the creative bodying-forth of "significant form" to be accounted for. And what is needed for this purpose is a pattern of interpretation which does not confuse origin with validity, which when it looks at art does not see something else instead, like ghosts of guilt or phantoms of fantasy, even though psychological determinants are very much in evidence.

Berdyaev's understanding of art in terms of creative transfiguring commends itself because it does not insist on reducing or dissolving the aesthetic into the psychological. It does need to be used with critical reserve, however. This kind of interpretation is wedded to a traditional conception of beauty which prevents it from responding positively to contemporary works in which the older category is either simply not relevant or denied altogether. Hence Berdyaev sees contemporary art, for the most part, as violating the canons of true art, producing works in which not embodiment but disembodiment, decomposition, the breaking up of beautiful forms, is the chief characteristic. At this point we shall have to part company with Berdyaev. We shall be leaning more toward truth as defining the functioning intent of artistic creation rather than beauty or goodness in their traditional usage. In following out this clue we shall be coming closer to the arts of today than Berdyaev is able to come. But his insistence that in art we have to do with God-given potentiality to create, and that there is an undeniable common ground between human creativeness and the divine creation, will be gratefully accepted and utilized in the following pages.

II

The bodying-forth that is achieved in art is not sheer miracle occasioned by ecstatic possession. It occurs in time as artists become craftsmen, gaining little by little mastery over a medium, learning to use tools and to perfect skills. Often it involves apprenticeship to a more expert worker, possibly even imitation of his style and methods. Training, discipline, repeated failure, renewed effort, patient learning from others as one keeps digging at "what lies under, lies under the shell"—all this is necessary and valuable. Artists grow restive under this necessity, not unnaturally, but they know that the discovery and release of one's own "native idiom" depends upon it. Abundant testimony may be found in such sources as the *Journals* of André Gide or Van Gogh's letters to his brother Theo.

There is such a thing as tradition in the arts, romantic notions to the contrary notwithstanding. Ways of perceiving and working are handed down; everything does not have to be learned all over again; artists go to school in order to acquaint themselves with styles already formed, finding affinities and models for their own developing métier. And their work is no less creative on that account, but more so. A young poet finds that there are conventions, stylistic options, expressive patterns with which he must sooner or later come to terms. A ballad is not a sonnet; decisions must be made as to the fitness of a form for what the poet is trying to say. Every selection means a discarding of what either doesn't need saying now or has been better said before. Creativity, then, should not be confused with utter novelty. It is the result of interaction between old and new forms, individual impulses and cultural patterns, freedom and tradition.

Not long ago a group of painters announced their intention to "create" by doing away with all preconceptions; they would have nothing in their minds when they started to work. They wished to do something entirely, stunningly new. As it happened this particular group made use of bits of corroded metal, driftwood, wire, and garden hose all cemented together on a two-dimensional surface. Instead of exhibiting a vacuum of preconceptions this group only succeeded in revealing what their preconceptions really were. They had something to say about the artistic possibilities inherent in bits of broken matter, and they said it forcefully, if not persuasively.

"It is always at the call of living forms that dead forms return to life." Thus André Malraux states the primacy of the creative element even when imitation or repetition are also present.[4] And we really cannot do without this stress, although we rightly shun a too absolutistic interpretation of artistic creativity. Not rupture with tradition as such, but freedom in the use of tradition is what makes a work of art creative; and

[4] In *The Voices of Silence* (New York: Doubleday, 1953), p. 66.

artists have and prize this freedom. Neither *de novo* nor *ex nihilo,* art nevertheless requires that it be understood as the embodying of "the forms of things unknown" through a power working in us that is singularly akin to God's own.

Let us call this human power "imagination." In giving it this name we are gathering up in one word a whole throng of meanings which seem at first to have very little in common. There is imaginary as opposed to real, and image as the mirror or copy of reality. To imagine is to dream up, fancy, idealize, realize, improvise, or reflect. What sense can be made out of such a plethora of meanings? And why bother anyway?

The answer is that a Christian understanding of the human imagination is long overdue. Is Shakespeare right, or is St. Theresa, who called imagination "the fool in the house"? Has analytical psychology demolished once and for all the claim of works of the imagination, made at least implicitly, to extend the range of our experience, kindle our sympathies, lengthen in time the span of lived reality, bring freshness and warmth of apprehension into our familiar orbits of observation and encounter? Do we not have instead, in what has been called imagination, a wild array of mechanisms and syndromes better termed "projection," "fantasying," "defense," "escape," and the like?

Not all imagination is regarded as pathological, of course. The most general psychological definition regards imagination as essentially the recombination of mental images of past experiences in new patterns; and perhaps this is as good a place as any to start. The capital point is that imagination is both a way of seeing and a way of making; borrowing a current term from sacramental theology, it is a re-presenting, or making present again. This function is by no means confined to the arts, for scientific inquiry affords many illustrations of it too. Compare, for instance, Poincaré's description of mathematical thinking with Van Gogh's report of artistic endeavor, and the similarities are striking.[5] In the arts, however, imagination is not only instrumental but intentional and is explicitly bound up with the end result as well as the way of working itself.

Stephen Spender stays close to the psychological view. He writes:

It is perhaps true to say that memory is the faculty of poetry, because the imagination itself is an exercise of memory. There is nothing we imagine which we do not already know. And our ability to imagine is our ability to remember

[5] See Julius Portnoy, "Is the Creative Process Similar in the Arts?" *Christian Faith and the Contemporary Arts,* Finley Eversole, ed. (Nashville: Abingdon, 1962), p. 59.

what we have already once experienced and to apply it to some different situation.[6]

But Richard Kroner adds a needed emphasis when he asserts that "imagination is not reproductive but productive. It does not copy the world we have perceived and experienced but transforms this world; it generates a world of its own." [7] The two judgments are not as far apart as they first appear, for memory itself is transforming, rather than being mere recall, and any "world of its own" which art may be said to generate will at least resemble that already experienced in some significant respects. It is as true to say that memory is a function of imagination as to put this statement in reverse. "Making present again" is a seeing-making activity in which new and old are firmly joined together.

Wherever its materials may come from and however they may be deployed, the artistic imagination is essentially a fashioning and shaping one, and hence is creative in the biblical, Christian sense. It is not a special kind of human activity disclosed only in what are conventionally termed the fine arts, since it is also

[6] In his essay, "The Making of a Poem," *Creativity in the Arts,* Vincent Tomas, ed. (New York: Prentice-Hall, 1964), p. 44.

[7] *The Religious Function of Imagination* (New Haven: Yale, 1941), p. 5.

evident in play or in the use of language; but in the arts it reaches a relatively high degree of intentional explicitness.

I believe that the creative imagination, as manifested in the arts, has a threefold aspect which is strikingly akin to the trinitarian understanding of God in the Christian faith. This similarity has been noted by Dorothy Sayers and others.[8] What Miss Sayers calls "the image of the Father" is the creative idea or vision in which a work of art may be said to begin. It is the creator's image of his own work, "complete at once, . . . the end in the beginning." It may be changed as the work proceeds so that what is created is quite different from what the artist originally planned. Yet the artist, as human creator, remains above his work by virtue of the fact that he is before his work, giving it such life as it has. By the image-making power which informs his work, he is also given control over it; in imagination he both transcends and becomes immanent in his work.

"The image of the Word," or Son, is found in the creative energy or activity which is the very working of

[8] Dorothy Sayers, *The Mind of the Maker* (London: Methuen, 1941); see also W. H. Auden, "The Dyer's Hand," *The Anchor Review, No.* 2 (New York: Doubleday Anchor Books, 1957), pp. 284-85; and Howard Boardman, "The Arts and Human Communication," unpublished paper.

the work. This is what we have called embodiment or bodying-forth; and it proceeds in time and space by imaginative concentration which achieves a unity of impact and impression, a concrete visibility or audibility, and yet a suggestive, evocative power of appeal or claim as well. The work thus produced is not only word, but word made flesh. In its separate existence it is independent of its creator, as it has perceivable shape and wholeness of its own; but as it is altogether dependent upon his creating, it is also the medium through which the creator may be known. Long after the creator has died his creation lives on, giving him a kind of immortality as real as it is strange. It is even a fair question to ask whether an artist is not himself more in his work than in his own life.

"The image of the indwelling Spirit," to continue with Miss Sayers' analogy, is the creative dialogue which is called forth by the work as encountered by others than its creator. The meaning engendered by lively response is not uniform but diverse, often amazingly so. My response to a work of art cannot be compelled. I may have come to the concert hall against my will, but the music I hear cannot move or please me involuntarily. I must give my consent to what is happening if it is going to happen for me. Whether I delight in what is being played or am repelled by it or find it merely boring, my response is free, which is only to say that it is mine. This power of creative interaction which is elicited by works of art cannot be analyzed, but only confessed. It is a kind of reverberation set loose in the world by the embodiment of the artist's vision. The artist hopes for it, his work bespeaks or claims it, and yet like the Spirit it "blows wherever it will." In contrast to the work and its creator such response cannot be located or fully explained. Yet its possibility is an intended aspect of the work itself, and it becomes actual as the perceiver or listener is personally drawn into the experience of having sensibilities awakened and reverberating to the reality before him.

It is clear that imagination is the common feature underlying this threefold mutation in the process of artistic creation and response. In imagination the work is conceived; by imagination it is embodied; and with imagination it is seen, read, heard, responded to inwardly. From first to last, art is imaginative, image-building, image-conscious. It is man's use of what God has given him to disclose and embody the meaning of his creaturely, yet creative, life.

Christianity, especially Protestantism, has to overcome a long and stubborn heritage of distrust of the imagination. The general tendency within the modern period has been to scorn or shy away from all imaginative renderings of human experience except those which might readily be assimilated to Christian purposes of instruction or edification. The more creative the imaginative work, the more suspect has been its motivation or effect. In part, perhaps, this general suspicion may seek justification in the ancient Hebrew horror of idolatry with its spurning of all "graven images" of the holy or divine. But modern Christian iconoclasm has other and less worthy sources—the pietism and moralism that have warped and distorted the gospel itself, as well as the liberalism and literalism which in contrasting ways have all but emasculated our faith. There have been great Protestant artists, but far too few of them. The makers of images have either felt alienated from the churches or have rebelled against the theologically trivial view of the arts and the imagination which has prevailed in them.

What is called for in our own day, therefore, is nothing less than the redemption of "the whole fateful realm of symbols and the life-meaning determined by them . . . the purification of the word or image," [9] indeed the

[9] Report of the Special Committee on the Council's Role in the Field of Religion and the Arts, National Council of Churches, p. 12.

baptizing of the imagination itself. An important part of this task is the effort to attain a better, truer understanding of what it is that constitutes religious and Christian art.

III

The recent discussion of these questions by theologians has, I think, been unduly dominated by Paul Tillich's distinction between explicitly and implicitly religious art. While Tillich did have a significant point to make, namely that religious value in works of art is not necessarily tied to those which have recognizably religious subject matter, he nevertheless left us without real guidance in judging what religious art truly is. "Ultimate concern" is neither a false nor an irrelevant principle, but it is an unfruitful one for exercising discrimination—especially when Tillich's own decided leanings toward aesthetic expressionism cause him to confuse ultimacy of concern with concern for ultimacy. A distinction between religiously conventional and religiously profound art is entirely proper and valid; but it is not identical with that between traditional and modern styles, as Tillich seems to hold, or at least as his examples suggest.

We do need to be shaken loose from the notion that it is subject matter alone that makes a work of art religious, and yet it does not follow that explicit treatments of religious themes are somehow less expressive of ultimate concern than those in which the religious aspect is only implied. The fact that a work is called a Nativity or a Crucifixion decides nothing one way or the other. It may be momentous and moving or merely trite and insipid. Still less, however, does the absence of religious subject matter guarantee depth of religious arousal and response. Again, that may or may not be the case.

There is no good reason why an explicitly religious art, like the poems of George Herbert or the biblical drawings of Rembrandt, should fail to be implicitly religious as well. Such works as these have both the burden of saying what is expected and the privilege of saying it afresh. When Rembrandt first began to use religious subjects in his work he simply drew upon them in the manner of his time as occasions for exercising his great skill. But in his later work these same subjects were treated with more penetrating insight, largely due to his own sustained study of the Bible. The line between explicit and implicit had vanished. Art and faith were creatively, memorably brought together in his mature work.[10]

[10] See W. A. Visser 't Hooft, *Rembrandt and the Gospel* (Philadelphia: Westminster, 1958).

We know that the choice of religious themes is no protection against banality or superficiality, and that works of so-called art which have these characteristics do a great disservice to authentic faith. When the treatment is such as to banish or ignore all mystery or to gloss over the human doubt and anxiety which are so much a part of all religious searching, then the verities and profundities of genuine faith are distorted or degraded in favor of popular stereotypes and bland formulas. Probably the most familiar example of this cheapening process occurs in the commercially produced motion picture, with its inevitable orgy and torture scenes and its baffling mixture of prurience and inoffensive sentimentality. But the church's own use of the arts may and sometimes does reflect a similar insensitiveness to the peculiar burden and privilege of religious art. One does not need to be more than reminded of the Christmas pageants and the Easter extravaganzas which have only made the gospel trivial and ridiculous.

Yet this is not the final word to be said on so important a matter. There is such a thing as honest and significant church art, just as there is art on religious themes which manages to stir the human depths and to awaken the sense of that awesome Presence for which faith's name is God. One may gratefully enumerate a long list of examples from his own experience: Bach's Wedding

Cantata No. 140, the Jesse window at Chartres, the abstract painting of Alfred Manessier, the "divine poems" of Henry Vaughan, Stravinsky's Symphony of Psalms, and many, many more. We are by no means without encouraging models and guidance, both traditional and contemporary, for the task of fashioning works that body forth our profoundest faith.

Today, however, we are being told on every hand and can certainly see for ourselves that the springs of such a faith are dying up. Will not religious art therefore become more and more vestigial, retrospective, and irrelevant? Is there even an outside chance that any kind of rebirth of religious images may take place in a world which has learned to do very well without God? Or, if not very well, at least to do without? Contemporary man is undeniably secular man, and his descendants are likely to be even more so. Must we not then conclude with those troublers of our religious peace that religious art is already dead in principle, that it has no possible future, and that this is clearly a "good thing"?

The advocates of a more or less radical secularity deserve our close attention. They are telling us something which we really know already if we but look carefully at the signs of the times all around us and within us. If the future of God is bound up with the enterprise we have been calling religion, then God is going to have a hard time of it indeed. Thus the alternative is posed between honest secularity and dishonest religiousness, and we are asked to choose the first. That such a choice does exist and is being forced upon us cannot be denied. But some things tend to be forgotten in the flush of discovery and the heat of discussion, at once oversimplifying and confusing. One is that "secular" and "religious" do not constitute a contradiction in terms, because "secular" itself has been a definitely Christian word, signifying the withdrawal of spheres of life from religious control and interpretation. The very words have meaning only in relation to each other, and the meaning disappears when that relation is altogether broken.

More important is the fact that when "religious" and "secular" are used to designate contrasting life styles, or styles in art, very often they are simply being confused with the words "sacred" and "profane." Now that we are all secular, there will be nothing sacred any longer; or rather, everything will be sacred, which amounts to the same thing. So speak the secularists. But does not secularization as a cultural process always mean "desacralization"—that is, the shrinkage and gradual elimination of the sacred or holy? And does this not involve an unmistakable degree of profanation, whether implicit or explicit? So speaks the religionist. There is enough truth in each charge to give us pause, but that is about all.

Let us see if we can give a more comprehensive, balanced statement of the situation.

The sacred is not the religious, although the religious may be a mark or witness of the sacred. And the secular is not the profane, although the profane may be manifestly at work in the secular. Sacred and profane are two ways of being in the world, as Mircéa Eliade writes, whether that world is predominantly secular or emphatically religious in its total cultural orientation. There is no good reason why a person should not live in the midst of secularity with a keen sense of the sacred, just as one may also live among religious facts and values with mocking disbelief and sullen profanity.

Professor Eliade has shown how modern nonreligious man, aided and abetted by secularity, is led toward a profane interpretation of his life in the world.

> First . . . he refuses transcendence, accepts the relativity of "reality," and may even come to doubt the meaning of existence. . . . He accepts no model for humanity outside the human condition. . . . Man *makes himself*. . . . The sacred is the prime obstacle to his freedom. . . . He will not be truly free until he has killed the last god.[11]

[11] *The Sacred and the Profane* (New York: Harper, 1961), p. 203.

But this, says Eliade rightly, is a program that cannot be carried to a conclusion. The majority of the irreligious "still behave religiously, even though they are not aware of the fact"—superstitions, taboos, myths out of the ancestral past continue to operate, compounded with new ones that are being invented every day. This would-be profane man "forms himself by a series of denials and refusals, but he continues to be haunted by the realities that he has refused and denied." [12] In consequence he may repress all concern with the sacred, driving it back to greater depths; but it remains ready to be reactivated and reintegrated as through telling symbols man "opens himself" once more to sacred reality.

Since art lives by and for the making of symbolic images, its role in any possible renewal of the sense of what is sacred will be a crucial one. This raises unavoidably the question of a Christian art which may not be religious in some merely reminiscent sense, but may be able to achieve genuine symbolic breakthroughs in an obviously secularized world. What kind of an art would this be, and have we any intimations of it in the work that is now being done?

First let us say what we mean and do not mean by Christian art. A work is not Christian merely because it is done by a Christian artist; that would be like saying

[12] *Ibid.*, p. 204.

that one's suit is Christian because it was made by a Christian tailor. Neither is a work Christian because the purpose for which it is intended is Christian; that would be like saying the furnace in the church basement is Christian because it is intended to warm Christians in the sanctuary above. Such factors as the allegiance and purpose of the artist are certainly part of the *provenance* of a Christian work, and yet they do not alone make it Christian. Something further is required—but what?

A work of art is Christian if it bodies forth and so conveys or opens up the gospel to men and women of any age or place. It is Christian if, and only if, the revealing and reconciling action of God in Jesus Christ informs it *ex opere operato,* as it were. A work of art does not have to be an ostensible representation of the gospel in order to be Christian, but it must in some degree make the gospel *present* again, entering the stage of our life in the world and addressing us as the human beings we are.

Must Christian works of art be things of beauty? Etienne Gilson thinks so, insisting upon retaining what for many contemporary artists has become quite an optional category. Only what is beautiful can rightly and truly praise God or celebrate his glory, affirms Gilson. But beauty has been analyzed to death, and is a word to stumble over. If it must be used in connection with works of Christian art, let it be in the sense given by Eric Gill: "Beauty is *the Splendor of Being.* The primary constituent of visible Being is Order."[13] If beauty means that which is pleasing, ennobling, or edifying, then it can hardly be applied directly or positively to the re-presenting of the gospel for people of our time. Indeed, when this aim dominates artists who like to think of themselves as doing a Christian work, we are more liable to get such cloying, mundane treatments as the heads of Christ by Hofmann or Sallman or the much greater but still not fully Christian Transfiguration of Raphael.

If the mystery of the gospel is to be conveyed to those of us who have our being in *this* world and not another, it will be through what Tillich has termed "broken symbols"—those which speak of God's loving deed in Christ not directly and confidently, but with refracted suggestiveness and glancing impact. One thinks here of *Billy Budd, Miss Lonelyhearts,* or the novels of Kazantzakis; of the church music of Flor Peeters and Jean Langlais; of Matisse's chapel at Vence and LeCorbusier's church at Ronchamp. All are, to my mind, powerful re-presentings of the gospel just because they

[13] In *Beauty Looks After Herself* (New York: Sheed & Ward, 1933), p. 66.

keep its gracious, liberating truth almost hidden, in reserve. "Only a suffering God can help," in the often quoted words of Dietrich Bonhoeffer. Knowing this, Rembrandt could show us in his paintings of the adoration of the shepherds and the wise men that this tiny child in the cradle is the Savior of the world; and Rouault likewise could make Good Friday speak of Easter and light his Galilean landscapes with the radiance of a kingdom yet to come.

If the substance of Christian art is the re-presentation of the gospel, its styles may be as free and various as the ingenuity of man can devise. There simply is no one form that is proper or correct for conveying the meaning of what God does for us in Christ. Any cultural epoch will have its own preferences and rejections, its own tastes and distastes with regard to the array of styles both traditional and contemporary that are offered to it. And within that epoch there will be sharp disagreement as to which styles of the past or the present speak most truly, pertinently, or amply to the human condition. That is as it must be, for what art keeps up is not a coercive monologue, as André Malraux writes, "but a dialogue indefeasible by Time." What matters supremely, from the point of view of Christian art, is that God who has visited and redeemed the world in the incognito of Jesus Christ may be "remembered and known still" in every circumstance or context; that he who bodied himself forth in the form of a servant may become serviceable to us again and yet again for our good and his glory.

IV

The remaining pages of this chapter will be given over to some reflections on the arts of the church, addressed particularly to Protestants. Pretty generally the Protestant, as was said of St. Paul, has been "an artist who did not want to be such." His preaching or teaching has been rather more expository or exhortative than evocative; the plastic arts have served him rarely and then chiefly as "visual aids"; his edifices, music, and orders of worship have seemed to underplay the native verve and exuberance of artistic imagination, wishing to keep art in its place as instrumental to more important things. Protestant art, when it does take shape, very seldom "lets itself go" but has a modesty and restraint, even a hesitation, quite foreign to its Orthodox and Roman Catholic counterparts.

It is not that there is anything aesthetically wrong with Paul Revere's communion plate, a Swedish Lutheran Sunday morning service, or a Colonial meetinghouse in New England. On the contrary, these are genuinely satisfying and deserving of Christian praise.

They do convey, each in its own way, the meaning of the gospel. They bring undoubted dignity and earnestness and spaciousness into the worship of God. And yet something is patently missing—what we shall call in the last chapter of this book "art as celebration." Protestantism keeps the middle course; having neither fasts nor fiestas it does all things decently and in order, obeying the Pauline injunction almost to the letter.

So when we Protestants look back in history at Byzantine icons or Gothic stained glass we do not quite know what to make of them. Even if we grant that they are works of art, we find it difficult to accept them as works of faith. Do they not seem to us to be essentially decorative rather than illuminative, instrumental and not sacramental? Quite possibly this is due to the historical fact that Protestantism has depended very largely upon verbal communication of the gospel and is therefore embarrassed or uncomfortable in the presence of nonverbal symbols of divine disclosure. Hence in the current ecumenical encounter Protestants do not quite know what to make of Catholic and Orthodox ways of worship, treatments of architectural space or pictorial representation more sensuous in character, more generous in their utilizing of the creaturely, image-making propensities of mankind. Although we may not go about smashing organs and breaking stained-glass windows, as some of our Puritan and Reformed ancestors did, their ghosts still haunt us.

There have been attempts to overcompensate, of course. An overblown aestheticism has invaded affluent Protestantism, "enriching" services and "beautifying" churches. A "cathedral complex" has seized and victimized us. Earlier canons of sobriety and honesty have been violated right and left. God has been left without a witness. But religion has done well and prospered; that is what this overcompensating trend in Protestantism is actually saying to us.

The problem of all Christian art, not only what makes it Christian but how it can be done at all, is magnified and not lessened when we come to the arts of the church. The church has "a given charter, a steady preserve, an undismissable memory, a living tradition" to which its liturgy, architecture, painting, or sculpture must be faithful. Many in our day are suggesting that the church should be instantly ready to assume new shapes, to turn itself inside out if need be, that the world might be more radically encountered and more rightly served. "How the church can minister to the world without losing itself" is a question that is both pressing and profound. Part of the answer, surely, lies in the church's way of approaching and using the arts. What the church has to do is to convey the gospel, really convey it, and see that it is really the gospel which is being conveyed. A precarious but exciting balance should be kept between tradition and creativity, representation and new revelation, form and flexibility; and the arts are indispensable to this exacting task.

Authenticity in church art is not to be confused with mere recognizability. Imitation Gothic, Romanesque, or Colonial buildings have long been identified with organized Christianity. When built in our own time they may embody adequately the faith of earlier generations, but can they express ours? The chances, I fear, are very much against it. Such buildings may do other good and necessary things, but this they can do only inadvertently, and often devastatingly. The Methodist cathedral on the boulevard, the Christian Science meetinghouse on the green, just do not ring true as church art. What they represent is a frantic clutching at a heritage without earning or repossessing it.

Must all church architecture then be contemporary in style? Not necessarily, but let us say that it helps. The usual protest of the "but it doesn't look like a church" variety should not be taken too seriously, but just seriously enough. There have been many buildings, called "chicken coop contemporary" by one respected architect, which have nothing to commend them but the fact that they are new. A building ought to look like a church if that is what it is; but what *should* a church look like? Traditionalism alone cannot answer that question. The forms of the church may be as many and divergent as the shapes which the love of God assumes in the world. Yet there is also an obligation to speak the name of God aright and to point to the way in which he was revealed for us men and our salvation, "that the world may believe."

Fortunately the number of church buildings that achieve this goal is steadily increasing. There are more signs of life and hope in architecture than in any other branch of church art today. I have already mentioned LeCorbusier's church at Ronchamp, France, with its thick overhanging mushroom-like roof, its sturdy white walls against its sloping hill. Another truly inspiring example is St. John's Abbey church in Collegeville, Minnesota, one of the centers of the liturgical revival within Roman Catholicism. Its rough concrete, bearing the mark of the forms into which it was poured, the bell banner which serves as a front gate, the splendid baptistry, the central freestanding altar and much more, make this building fashioned out of shapes and substances we know and live with a remarkable habitation of the Most High rising out of our own world and speaking powerfully to it.

The two examples I have given are Roman Catholic,

which is not to suggest that Protestant church architecture is unworthy by comparison, but rather to insist that we have now entered an ecumenical situation in which our separated traditions have much to learn from each other, and much to give as well. In such a situation the Protestant principle that only God can speak of God needs to be complemented and corrected by the Catholic principle that now that God has spoken, everything may speak of him. John Calvin described the human mind as a continuously working idol factory. And so it is; but it is also God's own image endowed with power to reflect divine creation in the things that are made. Protestants then may enter the ecumenical situation not as borrowers and beggars in the realm of church art, but as people with traditions and styles which are important to the well-being of the church as a whole. As we move out toward a more sacramental, incarnational view of church art, we shall find the Catholic coming toward us in new stress on preaching, reawakened sense of congregational life, Bible study, vernacular liturgy, and many other ways. Out of this meeting will surely emerge some blending of styles and forms which will leave their mark upon the whole church, and most especially upon its arts.

Church music, too, offers extraordinary opportunities for the contemporary artist and performer, although these have not yet been realized as in architecture. This quite plainly is the church's fault to a very large degree. The time when musicians such as William Byrd, Bach, or even Vaughan Williams could compose music for the service of the church is long past. Why? Because the church has alienated or repelled musicians of the first rank by insisting that its music must be acceptable to the common run of congregations, raise no questions, challenge no prejudices, and maintain the status quo. The wonder is that so much fine work is being done, sung, and played in the churches at all. It is still true, however, that music in the church is generally far from meeting standards of artistic excellence despite the valiant and increasing efforts of a devoted few.

And what shall we say of the liturgical and decorative arts? They rightly have an auxiliary role, to be sure, and yet they should not be neglected but greatly encouraged. I have seen homecrafted stained glass in a midwest village church which recalled Malraux's metaphor for the art: "A mosaic that has found its place in the sun." I recall chalices and crosses of honest workmanship, dance dramas that were not mincing and contrived, dossal curtains that were all the more beautiful because they had been made by women of the congregation. All this is good, since the real enemy of style and taste in church art is the ready-made, commercial product which by confirming our poverty of Christian imagination reveals it unmistakably.

It is probably too much to hope that in the years immediately ahead the arts of the church will find new vigor and scope commensurate with their powers and our urgent need. In the days when art was the acknowledged handmaiden of the faith, its works expressed convictions and longings of an already accepted, elucidated Christianity. Today, on the contrary, when the arts have left the church, the problem is that of first establishing real contact and communication with them on behalf of faith. What Amos Wilder calls "mobilizing a vanguard" of people in these two separated communities of endeavor should have high priority. This will mean working rigorously within the churches to lift standards of usage, taste, and expectation through a major effort at self-education and by deliberate, repeated exposure to the best.

It is a valid principle that in order to fulfill its real function church art must first of all be art. This needs both recognition and rendition in the entire gamut of ecclesiastical activity, from planning a new church building to selecting a hymn for the Sunday morning service. The exercise of Christian discrimination, as Brother George Every calls it, in "taking forth the precious from the vile" is the first step. The actual work of the imagination, bringing disclosure and embodiment of Christian meanings to "the chambers of imagery in the heart," is a long second step.

The pregnant phrase of Dante, "Art is the grandchild of God," should be remembered and acted upon by the church. All things made by man reflect and body forth the One who makes all things, including man. Who knows this better than the church of Jesus Christ, whose memory and hope are centered in the broken symbol of the very manhood of the most high God?

III *Art* as *Vocation*

Having considered the work of art as a disclosure and an embodiment, we now turn to the artist himself. Here again it is not some psychological explanation of his inner motives that we are seeking, but a frankly Christian interpretation of the way of life he has chosen. For this purpose, it seems plain, only the word "vocation" will do. Other words come to mind, of course, as describing the artist's permanent and personal relationship to his work. One is "commitment"—a word with too many pious and moral connotations, especially to Protestants, to make it very useful in this chapter. A better word, if we were prepared to accept it, might be the French word *engagement.* It means being caught up, involved, in some sort of program or cause; as men like Sartre or Camus use the term, it has the connotation primarily of political responsibility.

Every artist has certain *engagements* and commitments; they may be confusing and even conflicting in their multiplicity. But it is not of these common human loyalties, shared by the artist with each of us, that we are thinking now. It is not the artist as a father or a citizen or a teacher or a consumer, but as the sort of man who finds his lifework in art who concerns us here. Is he in the Christian sense of vocation "called" to be an artist?

I

The question seems forthright enough, but it is not capable of being answered with simple directness. Especially if we go to artists themselves for their opinion on the subject, we get a curious impression of self-contradiction. Some, like Rodin, insist that "artists are the most religious of men." Others, like Franz Liszt, whose life was that of a spoiled priest and who never forgave himself for not becoming one, feel that a life in art falls somewhere short of a true vocation. There are artists like Michelangelo or Rembrandt who arrive only gradually at a fully, consciously Christian view of the artistic impulse. And there are still others who never find a Christian frame of reference useful for self-understanding at all.

The approach to the question, then, cannot be made by polling artists themselves as though we could devise a kind of spiritual questionnaire for the purpose. Rather, it must be made in a more roundabout manner, giving full weight to the wide variety of capabilities and loyalties to be found in any company of artists. Yet the question cannot be gainsaid if the task of giving a Christian interpretation of the arts is to be taken up in earnest. And there is evidence enough that problems of vocation do beset many men and women who give the major effort of their lives to making works of art, so that the question is neither external nor irrelevant.

Vocation means being "called" to a particular work. The word is a Christian one, or was before it became secularized into a synonym for "occupation" or "profession." It signified that God had, in his gracious providence, given each man his work to do so that he could see the will of God in it. Not the religious or churchly nature of the work itself, as in Roman Catholicism, but the "calling" of God in any kind of work, as in Protestant thought and practice, is the keynote of vocation. Does it make sense in this general understanding of human work to speak of the artist as having a vocation?

Yes, it does, and for several reasons. A first is the primary motivation of the artist, which is not to achieve favorable recognition with the public or to find a comfortable social berth, but to get his creative work done. A second is the often reported sense of "internal necessity," as the painter Wassily Kandinsky calls it, which is formed of personal drive, cultural belonging, and aesthetic loyalty. A third is the artist's need to find enduring significance in his own art, to relate himself through it to the nature of things; "doing a job" is not enough for him, but he must work out a kind of destiny. In these and other ways the artist seems characteristically a person with a sense of vocation or something very like it, not to be confused with the sense of compulsion on one side nor with the sense of mission on the other, but nevertheless indicating the appropriateness of a Christian interpretation.

At the same time one must be on guard against the habit of making too grandiose, Wagnerian claims for the artist's vocation. Nonartists are probably most often at fault in this respect: "Art is the revelation of the infinite in the finite" was said not by an artist but by a well-known collector in the course of an after-dinner speech. If an artist himself were to talk thus about his work he would quickly be suspected of pretentiousness and pomposity. Of course he might actually believe it, too, but the proof of his statement must be found in the actual effects produced by his work upon others.

True vocation means that doing and being are one in a man's relationship to his work. What he has to do is the expression of his unique way of being human, and his being takes its shape from what he has done or is doing. We can scarcely doubt that art is a vocation in this basic meaning of the term. "I *must* be a writer," says C.-F. Ramuz at nineteen. "What would you have me be doing?" replies Pierre Bonnard to a visitor who was surprised to find him at his easel, painting. The artist has a vocation because his style of work is or is fast becoming his style of life as well. He puts himself into his work, as we say, and out of his work is built the substance of his selfhood, the very kind of person he happens to be.

Characteristically, then, art is neither a job nor even a profession, but a true vocation. The doing of it claims the artist in a personally engrossing, wholly committed way. In our society, to be sure, works of art are usually done in the artist's spare time, despite other duties and involvements. Only after one's reputation is established and a market has been found in our economy can artists give their entire attention and energy to their art. Until then, it is the rule that works of art are created in the gaps of time and energy left over after the means of livelihood have been won. And yet whatever may be the economic circumstances of the artist, between him and his art the relationship is typically one that is intimate, permanent, and intensive. Whatever else he may do or have to do, art is his "real work," as he will usually insist.

II

The actual meaning of any vocation or "calling" is made clear in terms of the fundamental loyalty that motivates those who belong to it. Can such a basic motivation be identified within the arts? What is the artist's loyalty? There is a line in one of Robert Frost's poems which states the matter in a very general way, to be sure, but also with considerable suggestiveness: "I had a lover's quarrel with the world." Since it is frequently the "worldliness" of the artist that seems to come between him and the religious person, it will perhaps be useful to draw out some of the implications of Frost's line, granting of course the well-known hazards involved in such borrowing of poetry for other purposes.

One of the best efforts to put into words the meaning of Frost's illuminating line is found in the Report to the National Council of Churches, already cited in the preceding chapter. I shall quote from it at length because it is an admirable summing-up:

> The artist loves the world. And because he wants to penetrate to the world's secret he cannot be content with obvious, merely surface appearances. . . . This loving faithfulness to the world may cause the artist to be harsh; it certainly means that he must select. All selection is a reduction in order to specify the particular and the significant; and such a process necessitates what the quick look will call distortion. But this distortion is not perverse or without sober intent; it is a turning and a twisting and a peeling-back to the end that the artist may find and state some truer, deeper, fuller form by which to declare his love.
>
> From this immediacy in love the artist cannot tear himself loose. He is bound to the world. Whether he deals with the world in forms that are harmonious or dissonant, forms that disclose an ideal or a bitter vision, the bondage remains. And all his efforts are ultimately a kind of tender celebration.[1]

This statement is revealing in that it presses home the essentially worldly allegiance of the artist, an al-

[1] Report of the Special Committee on the Council's Role in the Field of Religion and the Arts, p. 6.

legiance which is not without a certain unmistakable ambivalence. Did not Baudelaire confess, "I am an exile in the imperfect"? Not sheer and simple identification with the world but rather what this Report calls "the anguished confession of his resolute love" is evident in the artist. It is as if the artist, like Jacob wrestling with the night angel, were to cry, "I will not let thee go, except thou bless me." The artist does have a quarrel with reality; it does not satisfy him as it is, or he would not be engaged in reshaping it. Yet the quarrel is that of a lover, not a stranger or an enemy; and what gives the struggle such poignant urgency is the fact that it takes place within a basic covenanted faithfulness, a deep resolve to hearken to what the world is really saying. The artist does indeed love the world despite the apparent stubbornness with which it may refuse to yield to his craft and notwithstanding the wounds and lesions it inflicts upon his sensitive spirit.

Art makes a distinction and knows the difference between appearance and reality in the world. In his *Journals* André Gide speaks of "revealing the clandestine underside of things," and such an intention is indeed fundamental to all art. Conventional ways of looking at things are helpful to a degree as they establish a quick and ready currency of communication between us. But the artist, just because he trains himself to look more closely and carefully, cannot rest content with merely conventional perception. He must cut through the surface noises, the visual clutter, the accepted molds for the conveying of experience, to reach a freshness of vision which selects out of the general haze a concrete focus for new seeing. Thus T. E. Hulme wrote of artistic creation as "a process of discovery and disentanglement," [2] by which a Constable, for instance, breaks the molds of landscape painting up to his time and influences the English and French schools in a decisive manner. Art, says Hulme, "must be always individual and springs from dissatisfaction with the generalized expressions of ordinary perception and ordinary language." [3]

In both these ways, then, the "lover's quarrel" goes on. For the artist's love is not simply an infatuation or there would be no need for art. We might say that he takes the world as he finds it, but what he finds is not left as it is. His selectivity has in it a degree of rejection no less than of acceptance; his creative reshaping of the tones or colors of his being in the world is as much pruning and judgment as it is appropriation.

Yet the worldly allegiance of the artist is primary and indubitable, just as it is after all their love which gives lovers something to quarrel about. This worldliness must

[2] In *Speculations* (New York: Harcourt, Brace, 1924), p. 149.
[3] *Ibid.*, p. 153.

be granted and understood, as it often stands like a stumbling block in the way of Christian appreciation and right evaluation of the arts. Do not the cohorts of a believing respectability regard love of the world as an unholy alliance that is tantamount, in the artist's case, to something very close to irresponsibility and immorality? Without evading the issue or explaining it conveniently away, it can still be said that it rests all too frequently upon a fateful misinterpretation, which is as untrue to the arts as it is injurious to the Christian faith.

Here only a sound theological perspective can be of basic help. It is our plain, proclaimed faith that the bodying-forth of God in Jesus Christ occurs in and for the actual lived reality of this world, not some other. Since it is in this unique event that Christians find the sovereign clue to the meaning of all events, what God has done and given in Christ becomes for us not only the heart of the gospel itself but also the way of seeing and living in the world. The world which "God so loved" claims from us a concurrent answering love.

This is because it is God's world, as the doctrine of creation maintains. Whatever else that means, and there are many meanings capable of being stated variously, it clearly does mean that what owes its existence to God cannot be other than good. Its goodness, to be sure, is more a gift bestowed than a credit earned; and yet it is not a hovering, evanescent quality but a solid and palpable one built into whatever exists. To say "creation" is to affirm the goodness of creation not as we would wish to have it but as it stands. The Christian faith is world-affirming, not world-denying, at its very core.

It is not our faith to hold that creation was once good but is so no longer. That would be to take with chronological literalness, not theological seriousness, the Christian story of God's dealings with his world. Goodness is not the only quality evident in the created order, and our faith has much to say—and very rightly—about the fact that sin and evil have entered into it. In his *The Imitation of Christ* Thomas à Kempis wrote that "all perfection in this life has some imperfection mixed with it, and all our light is not without some darkness." True enough; but lest his words be turned into an invitation to melancholy, due weight should be given to the balanced wisdom they contain. The accent surely is upon the goodness of creation, however much it may be compounded with or darkened by what is clearly not good. It is as true to say, then, that the world as we know it is a mingling of the imperfect with the perfect and that darkness is not altogether unrelieved by light. That in simplest terms is what the goodness of creation means.

Into this world, and not another fancied one, God was "pleased as man with man to dwell." That is the central fact concerning the relation of nature and grace which makes the Christian interpretation of the world possible and necessary. The incarnation is as much a statement about the world as it is about God; it is indeed the establishing of a new relationship between God and the world. That grace and truth came by Jesus Christ does not barely indicate the manner of their coming by making a claim of supremacy for Christ. What is also claimed is that grace and truth actually did come, are here to stay until the world ends, so that everything we call "world" is different because God entered it, en-manned in Christ. In the words of Brother Antoninus:

> God wrote the mark of liberation
> Everywhere on the wondering human face.

Henceforth this world with all its familiar shapes and energies is where our salvation must be worked out, albeit with fear and trembling. That it is also where we have tribulation goes without saying. But since our place and life in it has been made the fit habitation of the world's Redeemer, the world is the theater of God's grace, the "divine milieu," as Teilhard de Chardin expressed it.

It is therefore this world, this sin-ridden yet redeemable world, which is given for our duty and delight. If it was good enough for God to dwell in we are not at liberty to despise it, out of supposed faithfulness to him. No doubt there are decisions to be made; our wills must be trained to true obedience; the created and redeemable goodness of the world does not imply that choices between better and worse are not necessary, nor that one thing is as good as another. Yet if God has given in Christ his unmistakable vote of confidence in his world, we who profess belief in him can do no less.

Very recently we have been hearing much in Christian circles about the worldliness of authentic faith. This is indeed a long overdue word. It may, however, come too late to repair the breach that has grown up between believer and artist. The plain fact is that workers in the arts quite regularly regard the Christians they meet with indifference, dislike, or outright hostility. Do the latter not seem to belong to another world, using this one as a stepping-stone to it? Do they not often view the artist's hard-won achievements with censoring disapproval or uncomprehending disdain? It may well be asked whether Christians have rightly heard the Word spoken in the mystery of Christmas and Easter, or have rather rendered it innocuous and unfruitful, sealing it up in a pageant-like realm of its own.

But he who creates and redeems the world does not intend that nature and grace, each with its partisans or devotees, should remain insulated and apart. In God's world nature is the environing of grace, as grace is the fulfilling of nature. Therefore Christian faith in its expressions of worship and witness must not ignore "the way things are" which is nature, and artistic seeing and making cannot long be impervious to the intimations of grace. Although we may, purely for the sake of semantic convenience, refer to grace and nature as separate realms or zones of being, it is signally important to know that they are given together, each meant for the other, in the Christian understanding of the world.

For God too, as we meet and know him in Christ, has a lover's quarrel with the world. His grace has been resisted and refused again and again, and yet it is continuously being offered. God is unwilling to take nature's *No* for a final answer, and so works lovingly upon it from within through the incognito of his healing and restoring Word. That Word in becoming flesh causes the flesh to become Word. Thus the whole creations waits, groaning in its travail, waits for the showing forth of the children of God.

III

The vocation of the artist, premised upon this deeply mysterious viability of the world, may be compared at certain significant points with the callings of the priest and the prophet. As we come upon these types of human fidelity to God in the pages of the Bible, they too are possessed by seriousness of purpose and strictness of life. There are false prophets and unworthy priests just as there are slovenly or frivolous artists; but when they are living up to the measure of their respective callings, doing work that is genuine and rings true, all are self-dedicated men.

This seriousness of the artist needs to be underscored, if only because his reputation as an irresponsible flouter of conventions or a basically self-centered person persists among those nonartists who find it possible to compare themselves favorably with him. It is of course true that art, if it is to become one's way of life, must liberate its devotee at least to some extent from the conventional orthodoxies and mythologies of the time and place which have been given him to work in; some he may treat with amused tolerance, others with abrupt impatience or contempt. His very break with convention, however, is a good measure of his seriousness in pursuing his own work; and his insistence on personal privacy may really be his only way of guarding and maintaining basic human integrity. To be "true to one's genius" is a goal that sometimes leads into strange bypaths of deviation from one cultural norm or another, but eccentricity among artists is seldom an end in itself. When it puts in an appearance, as it frequently does, nonconformity may be borne with patience, if not actually welcomed, so long as it indicates the seriousness with which an artist takes both his work and himself in relation to it.

G. K. Chesterton once said that the artist "exults in the sheer steeliness of steel and the unutterable muddiness of mud." Here is a further evidence that art like prophecy or priesthood is vocationally serious. The intent is to savor the very substance of a matter, to call attention to its essence, whether it be the folds of drapery rustled by the wind or the play of candlelight on satin or the look of suffering in the eyes of a dying man. Not even mud or steel give up their secrets easily for all the world to see. This takes a bit of doing, as the saying goes. An artist who binds himself to this discovering and disentangling of the really real has set a long and arduous course. To describe afresh and unforgettably the sound of marching feet in rhythmic language, to convey the song of angels on a piano keyboard—these are exacting, strenuous tasks requiring all the wit and skill that one can summon up. More, they demand a large degree of self-surrender, which is always the mark of true vocation in the terms of Christian faith.

In drawing a comparison between the artist and the priest and prophet of the Bible, attention is being called to a certain common stance in relation to culture. When that culture is unabashedly secular, as is our own, without visible means of external divine support, the role of the artist becomes that of the defender of man, not that of the mediator and proclaimer of God. Yet something of the priestly and the prophetic stance remains. Who else lifts up as the artist does the values deeply cherished in his social world, or who can be so depended upon to protest against the cheapening of life and the degrading of the human?

Insofar as artists take upon themselves these tasks, whether implicitly or explicitly, they may be regarded as priestly and prophetic in relation to their culture. Consider first the artist as a kind of priest, the celebrant of a people's treasured meanings and values. This is a role which many artists would refuse today, preoccupied as they are with defining themselves sharply against the prevailing winds of custom and doctrine shared by the majority of their contemporaries. Nevertheless the priestly role is filled, by whatever name it may be called, whenever an artist is able to burnish a common truth until it shines, or succeeds in saying effectively for others what they cannot say for themselves. Although the contemporary artist seldom if ever thinks of himself as being the mediator of the sacred to his own people, he is actually engaged in finding substitutes for the sacred; he does in some sense want his truth to become everybody's truth; and like Albert Camus, he sees his art as "a means of stirring the greatest number of men by providing them with a privileged image of our joys and woes." [4]

Not all artists speak of their own work with the compelling lucidity of Camus, yet his words have commanded hearty assent among many of them. The culture we live in does not habitually look to the artist as a priest in the older biblical sense; that is true. It is perhaps of interest to note that the word "hieratic"—a synonym for "priestly"—is generally employed in modern criticism to describe art of a highly stylized, formal character, usually with a suggestion of the archaic, and preferably with a sense of the ominous or foreboding. That is about as far from Chaucer's priest or the country curé of Georges Bernanos as could be imagined. Solemnity is almost all that remains of the older and Christian meaning. The priests as representative man, as a stand-in for humanity, is a conception that has noticeably lost its hold as indicating the artist's role within his community.

However, the more ample meaning of priesthood is worth bringing back in this connection; it is even indispensable. In the work of art there is a taking up of

[4] *Speech of Acceptance upon the Award of the Nobel Prize for Literature* (New York: Knopf, 1958), p. viii.

the stuff of life, raising it to a higher power. Forms we encounter every day in blurred outline the artist makes visible to us in sharp relief. T. E. Hulme wrote in his essay on Bergson's theory of art:

> It is as if the surface of our mind was a sea in a continual state of motion, that there were so many waves on it, their existence was so transient, and they interfered so much with each other, that one was unable to perceive them. The artist by making a fixed model of one of these transient waves enables you to isolate it out and to perceive it in yourself.[5]

This lifting up of the common to the uncommon level, this brooding upon the initially insignificant until it becomes significant, first to the artist and then to others, may quite properly be likened to the action of the priest in sacramental worship. Even though an artist may consider himself to be a pagan celebrator of the godless, a devotee of the profane, he performs this service to his culture in a kind of parody of priestly action. He may not choose the office, but it is thrust upon him nonetheless by virtue of the very nature of his art.

Examples of the truth in this analogy are abundant. There is the poet Wallace Stevens saying, "In an age of

[5] In *Speculations*, p. 150-51.

disbelief it is for the poet to supply the satisfactions of belief, in his measure and in his style." [6] Or this from the critic Denis de Rougemont: "Art would appear to be like an invocation (more often than not unconscious) to the lost harmony, like a prayer (more often than not confused), corresponding to the second petition of the Lord's prayer—'Thy Kingdom come.'" [7] Or again, James Joyce, in many respects the most consciously priestly of all modern writers: "I imagined that I bore my chalice safely through a throng of foes." [8] In these instances, to which a great many more might be added, the essential priesthood of the artist is confessed.

It is easier to think of the artist in comparison with the prophet because the parallels are more obvious. Prophecy in its original sense meant speaking for God to one's people, usually in judgment and condemnation of the people's faithlessness. "Thus says the Lord" often prefixed what purported to be direct quotation from God, who presumably spoke Hebrew. It is not, however, in the manner so much as in the substance of biblical

[6] *Wallace Stevens: Opus Posthumous,* S. F. Morse, ed. (New York: Knopf, 1957), p. 206.

[7] "Religion and the Mission of the Artist," *Spiritual Problems in Contemporary Literature* Stanley R. Hopper, ed. (New York: Harper, 1952), p. 186.

[8] Quoted by Harry Levin, *James Joyce* (rev. ed.; New York: New Directions, 1960), p. 29.

prophecy that its echoes are to be heard in the arts of today. Very few artists would claim to be telling anyone what God had already told them. They are not as sure of God as the prophets were—which is a masterpiece of understatement—and of all things, they do not want their work to be confused with preaching.

Yet if this superficial resemblance is lacking, there are other and more profound similarities, even affinities. Something like the prophet Amos' plumbline measuring a warped and tottering edifice of culture is almost visible in the work of many major artists today. They do not like what they see about them; and since they see more sensitively than most of us, their reports of "a world gone awry" are sobering and deserve respect. Fernand Léger, for example, paints "Three Women" at what at first seems to be a tea party but soon takes on the characteristics of a factory interior. The women themselves are gross, robotlike, vacuous. His canvas itself would probably be described by Ortega y Gasset as illustrative of "the dehumanization of art"; but what Léger makes visible is the dehumanization of man—or in this case, of woman. The very unreality and unlikelihood of the scene is the signature of the artist's prophetic fervor. He really cares about this and is asking us to change our way of life. His work speaks for itself, but speak it does.

Or take the married couple, George and Martha, in Edward Albee's play *Who's Afraid of Virginia Woolf?* Of them one critic has remarked: "They are, in short, a sort of regurgitative projection of all that is despicable in man—human beings without pity . . . except for themselves; and they interest us only because they appeal to our curiosity concerning the abnormal. We used to go to the circus to see freaks; today we go to the theater." [9] True enough; but what if this disgust is just what the playwright intended to arouse? Mr. Albee can scarcely be faulted for not giving us characters to admire if his bitter vision is to make itself felt in the theater. He does, after all, have something unpleasant to say, and it cannot be said pleasantly.

This fact alone does not make Mr. Albee a prophet, of course; there is even a legitimate question as to whether the inducing of disgust is a proper aim of dramatic and theatrical art. The point is that the playwright or the painter would not put on exhibition these displeasing symbols of our condition if they did not want to displease us. Highlighted, oversimplified, exaggerated as these symbols may be, they serve a purpose which at least reminds us of the prophetic art of an Ezekiel or a Hosea, both of whom found similar ways of disturbing

[9] R. H. Gardner, *The Splintered Stage* (New York: Macmillan, 1965), p. 152.

the conscience and troubling the self-understanding of their people.

It is fairly clear that this sort of prophetic impulse is at work among many artists in our time. They wish to expose and exhibit whatever is false, pretentious, hollow, or cheap. They declare judgment upon indifference and unconcern. When they see signs of disorder and disintegration, particularly in the human realm, they do not hesitate to say so. Instead of talking about the breakdown of human communication, for example, they simply break it down for us to see and hear, like Beckett and Ionesco in the "theater of the absurd." Whether through satire, fantasy, or apocalypse, their work yields a knowledge of ourselves, which when rightly received is "carried to the heart," in William Faulkner's words.

This may be prophecy, someone is bound to say at this point, but is it art? The question, although it is so hypothetical as to be almost irrelevant, is frequently asked. The answer is that one can only see what is there to be seen, can only disclose to others what has been disclosed to him. There is in principle no reason why moral indignation or spiritual despair may not serve as creative stimuli quite as effectively as do experiences of serenity and positive assurance. Moreover, is it not true that we often learn best what something means by taking a hard look at its opposite? The person who has felt the sharp edge of injustice is the one who knows what justice really is. He who has been dealt with unmercifully cries out most earnestly for true mercy. Is there any form of radical protest which is not also at bottom an affirmation? Let it be granted that a work of art should be judged and responded to on its own terms, aesthetically, but those whose complacency has never been disturbed by the artist can scarcely even know what he is about.

Often, especially in the greatest art, what we have been calling the priestly and the prophetic impulses merge. They seem to reinforce each other in aesthetically interesting and valid ways. One may perhaps be dominant while the other is recessive, or latent while the other is quickly apparent. When an artist gives fair warning that his truth is going to hurt, portrays human nastiness with compassion, or mingles biting scorn with sympathy, his work is strangely analogous to the words of judgment and reconciliation spoken together in Christian faith. In Camus' telling phrase, the work of art "does homage to the wretched and magnificent life that is ours." [10]

[10] Albert Camus, *Resistance, Rebellion, and Death* (New York: Knopf, 1960), p. 239. This quotation and the form of the section above, I owe to Roger L. Shinn, "The Artist as Prophet-Priest of Culture," *Christian Faith and the Contemporary Arts*, pp. 72-79.

IV

And so we come around once more to the central matter of this book. In what I have called the deepening dialogue between faith and art, to speak of analogies, affinities, or similarities is all very well. However, it says really very little unless it leads to an actual rendezvous of mutual understanding and support. There is no virtue in trying to conceive art and faith as two separate things between which some kind of relation may be said to exist. These terms themselves are but shorthand expressions standing for certain ways men have of doing and being—ways that meet and part, now attract and then repel each other, but are nevertheless bound up together in the bundle of our common cultural life. My thesis here is simply that these ways may be seen to come together in the artist's own vocation, as we traced their convergence earlier in his works.

One theme that exerts considerable fascination upon those who study the arts knowingly and thoughtfully is that of the artist as a kind of saint. Men like Jacques Maritain, Amos Wilder, and Etienne Gilson have found it illuminating to employ the category of sainthood as an *entrée* to the meaning of artistic vocation. Gilson, for example, gives the following citations from three quite dissimilar men of letters. From C.-F. Ramuz: "The artist and the saint are one and the same. Self-sacrifice, world renunciation, acceptance of insult and privation, states of grace, a rule, disciples. . . . The truths of the Gospel transferred to aesthetics, so to speak." Or this from Oscar Wilde remarking that "while metaphysics interested me very little and morality not at all, there was nothing in the teachings of Plato or Christ that could not be directly transposed to art and find there its perfect fulfilment." And André Gidé: "It amazes me that no attempt has ever been made to draw out the *esthetic* verity of the Gospel." [11]

These writers are not offering a casual suggestion that an interesting parallel may be drawn between two types of human endeavor and excellence generally supposed to be quite different. They are asking for Christian recognition and interpretation of their own vocation. In this respect they are representative of a large and impressive group of modern artists who claim that their vocation should be seen and welcomed as a service pleasing to God. They give an affirmative answer to the question asked by Gerardus van der Leeuw, "Can art be a holy act?"

Such artists do not pretend to be better than they are; they make no claim to moral perfection, with which

[11] Gilson, *Choir of Muses* (New York: Sheed & Ward, 1953), pp. 185-86.

sainthood is widely and wrongly confused. Yet they feel a kinship with the saint which they would like to see reciprocated. Although they do not think of themselves as being concerned with the proclamation of the gospel, they ask that art be illumined by the light of the gospel. Surely such a plea is important and deserves Christian consideration and reply.

Sainthood, of course, is not a vocation corresponding to others; it is capable of coexisting with many and is confined to none. Especially, it is not to be identified with religious performance or preoccupation, although it is entirely natural that institutional religion should pay tribute to the saint and wish to foster and emulate his quality of spiritual life. The saint, in fact, is something of a mystery not only to the world at large but also to the church itself. Neither world nor church quite knows what to make of human characters so exceptional, so difficult to analyze or classify within the general run of mankind.

It is not that the saint is necessarily a nonconforming rebel, though he sometimes may be. Usually he arouses admiration rather than disapproval among those who know him. He may be thought impractical but he is seldom regarded as dangerous or wrong-headed, except by those of pedestrian bent who are easily intimidated by excellence in any form. What genuinely puzzles people and occasions not a little envy is the saint's evident freedom from the mad scramble, the snarls and tangles of ordinary existence. He appears to possess some kind of secret that lifts him above the battles for survival and status. His life is not lived on the customary surface. His spirit, it seems, responds to a different and more distant music. The springs of his action and allegiance are not obvious, but hidden. The saint is baffling to the majority of men in his astonishing power of concentration, in his intense detachment, in the courage with which he follows through his vision.

One might therefore almost define the saint as an artist of the spiritual life, since these same qualities are much in evidence among artists. Father Louis Lavelle accordingly writes of the saint's "unwavering vision," his "going to the limit" in the use of his powers, and his "standing at the frontier" of the material and the spiritual.[12] The life of the saint becomes his own creative disclosure and embodiment of the grace of God which in Christ has been let loose in the world.

St. Francis of Assisi comes immediately to mind as an example of the artist-saint. Many have tried to lay bare his secret. What constitutes the perennial and universal appeal of his extraordinary spirit? Perhaps an answer

[12] In *The Meaning of Holiness* (New York: Pantheon, 1954), pp. 3-12.

may be found precisely in what is so elusive and therefore so endlessly fascinating. On the one side, renunciation, austerity, strictness of life; on the other, expansiveness, joyous abandon, gusto, and a tingling delight in being alive in the world. As Lavelle observes, thinking of Francis, "As soon as man diverts his gaze from himself he has the whole of nature before his eyes." [13] Thus between the two sides there is a close, even organic relationship; there is not the strain and paradox which some on either side profess to make out. Giotto, whose paintings were inspired by St. Francis, perfectly portrays the world of Franciscan spirituality. It is a world mysteriously gracious, refreshingly familiar in which nature is neither scorned nor adorned, but transfigured and, as it were, ensouled.

It can scarcely be denied that some have been attracted to the Franciscan vision only aesthetically, responding eagerly to the delicacy of detail and the picturesque humanizing of natural objects and forces while ignoring everything marked by saintly rigor and deprivation. This may be regarded as unfortunate, but it does not justify our calling the aesthetic response either unwarranted or inappropriate. That which is admirable ought to be admired. While it is true to say with Lavelle that "spiritual life perishes if it is reduced

[13] *Ibid.*, p. 34.

to the level of aesthetics," this does not forbid all aesthetic appreciation of spiritual insight or meaning. When a movement like that initiated by St. Francis has a profoundly creative effect upon the arts, it is an occasion for Christian gratitude and appropriation.

One gets a bit weary of hearing spokesmen for the Christian faith speak in a superior way about art and the aesthetic experience. Is it really a question of "reducing" what is spiritual to some supposedly lower aesthetic level? By what right does faith presume to rank or value orders of experience relative to its own primacy? Even if Kierkegaard or Kant said so, must it be assumed that the types of human knowing and doing crystallized in art and faith are necessarily incompatible or await some sort of synthesis on a "higher" level? It is by no means clear that the transposing or transferring of the gospel into symbolically efficacious terms involves a diminution or distortion of its saving power. Indeed, such a transference is the very condition of the hearing and obeying of the gospel and occurs in every act of worship, every sermon, every teaching or witnessing situation where a genuine breakthrough is established. Is it not therefore rather a question of raising, not reducing, truths of the spirit to the level of aesthetic expression and encounter?

What one suspects is that this rather lofty attitude toward the arts has its uneasy anchorage in a twofold misunderstanding. First, aesthetic experience is assumed to be a passive beholding rather than a passionate involvement which as "everyone knows" today is the sign of true faith. Second, there is the old prejudice against art as something playful, lacking sobriety and responsibility, rather than seeing it as the purposeful, dedicated enterprise it generally is. Underneath much that passes as theological critique of the arts there seems to be this sort of judgmental moralism and activism, together with an inability to let go and to be moved by what is humanly significant unless it meets tests laid down in advance. On such terms any real dialogue is plainly impossible.

Without wishing to belabor the point unduly, let it simply be pointed out that those who thus seek to prove their zealous devotion to "spiritual things" are sadly lacking in Christian generosity. Doctrinal standards we must have, of course; but they may not be so different from aesthetic criteria as is often supposed. There can be no merit in assuming that art must content itself with providing illustration for faith. There is even less in supposing that theology is in any position to give its imprimatur, or the opposite, to works of art. No such accreditation is required in order to make art a holy act.

What then is required? In asking this question we come face to face with the whole matter of "inspiration."

Is this only another of those formerly Christian but now thoroughly secularized ideas which no longer merit serious theological attention? Or may it on the other hand be worthy of Christian restatement and restitution?

"I never had a choice," wrote Nietzsche, thinking of the writing of his own *Thus Spake Zarathustra*. This involuntary quality which Joachim Konrad calls "passivity and constraint" [14] is characteristic of artistic inspiration. The phenomenon itself is indubitable, but artists and critics constantly debate its meaning, some emphasizing inspiration as ecstatic possession with others stressing its unconscious or even manic origins. To be inspired is not merely to be used by a blind automatic process but to be caught up and carried along by a creative impulse or suggestion which is then developed or elaborated in the finished work. Whether the inspiration takes place only at the beginning or whether it operates throughout the making of a work of art, it is a frequently reported experience. But what is its source? The artist is right in being troubled by this question. He wants and needs to know if he is truly a discoverer or only an inventor. Does he merely yield to some obscure but powerful pressure of his own feelings, or is he answering a call from somewhere else?

[14] In *Religion und Kunst* (Tübingen: Mohr, 1929).

The notion given currency by the Romantic poets that inspiration unconsciously produces works of art cannot stand up under careful scrutiny of the works themselves. Anyone who has studied the rough draft of a poem by Wordsworth or the notebooks of Leonardo da Vinci knows better. Yet the view that consciously controlled art can generate an inspiration is equally unsound, for as Plato reminded us in speaking of the poet, "there is no invention in him until he has become inspired." To be sure, an artist may take a long time to find out what his inspiration is; a ready-made inspiration would be an absurd self-contradiction; "hard deeds, the body's pains," much skill and perseverance, are necessary, for we do not call a great work of art a masterpiece without reason. All the same, inspiration is the one thing needful if such work is to be brought into existence. Without it, labor is useless and study is vain; what Paul Valéry called a "gift of the gods" must come first, or there is nothing to be elaborated or developed.

Here as before we see the psychologist barring our way, for "inspiration" is not a word in his vocabulary and he believes that what it means can be better explained than by reference to gods or Muses or any sort of capturing higher powers. He finds it highly significant that the experience called inspiration has been traditionally linked to madness; he tends to view it as a symptom of disruption and disorder rather than as a source of creative order. Thus there is a definite obstacle to communication between the artist's own self-understanding and the explanation of it offered by psychology. Ben Shahn's words on this subject are worth quoting:

> The subconscious may greatly shape one's art; undoubtedly it does so. But the subconscious cannot create art. . . . The psychological view can at best, even assuming that it were accurate, tell us what man is in spite of himself. . . . To the psychologist it is the periodic insanity of Van Gogh that is pre-eminent, and the psychologist deduces much from that. But to the artist it is clear that it was the great love of things and people and the incredible suffering of Van Gogh that made his art possible and his insanity inevitable.[15]

Although Ben Shahn does not speak here of inspiration, he insists that art becomes possible only through human intention and sympathy consciously felt and exerted. Reducing art to nonartistic terms does not "explain" it.

What then does account for the artist's often repeated testimony that he does not so much choose his work as the work chooses him? The claim to inspiration has an unmistakably Christian sound whether it is made by Christians or not. If and when the claim is a valid one,

[15] "The Biography of a Painting," *Creativity in the Arts*, p. 28.

it rests upon what in our faith is called the work of the Holy Spirit, God the Illuminator and Enlivener, "who with the Father and the Son is worshipped and glorified." In the truest sense an inspiration is not something to be claimed but rather to be confessed, since it means in Nietzsche's words that one is a "medium for overwhelming powers." How one wishes that Fra Angelico, like Pascal, had kept a record of his inspired moments! He must have had them, for his works have that lively and life-giving radiance which can only come from the Holy Spirit.

"I never had a choice." Here the artist sees himself enthralled, pressed into service, answerable to the source of his inspiration. His art is first a gift and then a duty. Whether he believes in God is perhaps not as important as the fact that God believes in him, choosing him for the despair and the delight of making Word become flesh. At all events that is the way in which a Christian would put the matter. It is no part of our faith that God must have proof of the conscious devotion of a human agent before he deigns to call him into service. The Spirit, like the wind, blows wherever it wills and takes possession of whomever it pleases.

In this respect the artist and the saint are, if not quite, almost one. For both of them vocation is the fundamental fact of life; and for both it takes the form of servanthood, of serviceability to a mission and a witness in which they are asked to lose themselves. Although they cannot choose to be employed in this service, they can and do consent to being chosen and set at work. Thus each transposes and draws out the verity of the gospel, by whatever name it may be called, finding in its service his perfect freedom, and learning, as we shall see in the last chapter, to rejoice in its truth.

IV Art as Celebration

There is a difficulty about the topic of this chapter which may as well be laid bare at the beginning. To speak of art as celebration is to think at once of corporate rejoicing or remembrance, perhaps a ceremonious public occasion or a more intimate family gathering around a birthday cake or a Christmas tree. Such events are pleasant enough to think about, as happy and festive experiences always are; but what does all this have to do with art, especially contemporary art?

I

Even if it be granted that art in past ages had the character of celebration, can we seriously maintain that it does today? Generally speaking, it seems to be private rather than public in its origin and impact, and certainly far from joyous in either style or substance. Contemporary art, however strong it may be in its unsparing exposure of human wretchedness, is not widely noted for its capacity to arouse emotions of well-being or enjoyment. Instead, it typically awakens reactions of a much more negative sort ranging from discomfort to disgust. This at any rate is what those who claim to speak for the average viewer, listener, or reader are in the habit of asserting. Such art may indeed be most effective as a prescription for despair, but who would have the temerity to call it celebration?

The problem is a real one and cannot in honesty be ignored. It is true that many artists in our day have become preoccupied with what is broken, deviant, or malignant in man's existence—so preoccupied that their work has taken on a tone of unrelieved hopelessness. Yet it is also true that multitudes of people who ought to be attending to what the arts are saying prefer not to see or hear. No one likes to be brought up short or shocked into recognition of the ugly or unpleasant facts of life. Has not art been until quite recently the realm of the beautiful and the sublime? Hence many people still turn to works of art for relief and reassurance, and are disappointed when these benefits are not forthcoming. Not wishing to be disturbed, they refuse to become involved or moved, and the artist is driven to even greater lengths of stridency or overstatement in order to break through their indifference.

By reacting in this way to contemporary artists and their work we deny ourselves a far more precious boon than beauty—we insulate ourselves against the truth which they would share with us. The human picture to which they draw our attention is not a pretty one and it cannot be made prettier than it is. And yet, as Joseph Sittler observes, strange heavens of vision and accomplishment are being formed in unbelievable hells today; a work of art in this or any other time represents a surmounting of obstacles, a fashioning of order from disorder, a "spell against death." As such it is a cause for celebration whether we find it personally attractive or not. So long as man is able to expend his energies in artistic creation, he need not be an object of despair. If, like the artist of today, he can wrest communicable meaning out of apparent meaninglessness or bring our darkness onto a lighted stage, he deserves both gratitude and respect.

Art, then, is worthy of being celebrated solely as a human achievement; but is art itself a celebrating of life? Yes, inevitably and always, though by different tokens and in differing measures. *Ex opere operato,* by virtue of the work being worked, art is an act of celebrating life. That may not be its all-controlling purpose or its ostensible occasion, yet celebration is bound up with the very idea of art and its execution, as it is tied, more obviously perhaps, with the publication, performance, or exhibition which eventuates. Objectively art is celebration, the singling out and lifting up of something the artist feels has durable and shareable worth, whatever may be the subjective texture of the work in subject matter, emotional impact, or motivation. The greater the art, the more this is true of it. Yet the same truth holds for every work of art regardless of the mood or effect it produces, from a Scottish ballad to a Bach fugue, or from the rock sculpture in an Indian cave to Brancusi's marble birds in flight.

To be sure, the celebrative nature of all art is often repressed or given a sardonic turn in present-day art.

One thinks, for example, of a canvas painted black on which, as the eye grows accustomed to the blackness, a tiny white patch appears. Or Sartre's play *No Exit* comes to mind, in which three characters torture the truth out of each other in a closed room that seems to be hell, until a door opens which no one makes a move to go through; the real meaning of the play's title is not that there is no way out, but that no one takes the available way. Thus possibility is introduced as judging actuality, presence is masked under the mode of absence, and passionate negation becomes by virtue of its very passion an affirmation.

That this is a new kind of language for communicating and so celebrating human truth in art no one can deny. It is, however, a language that can be learned and used, and one that comes home sometimes with more power than the glad recital of known joys or the glistening surfaces of what is at once pleasing and approved. In a time when we must perhaps be grateful for small favors the recognition of this muted character of celebration in the arts becomes especially important. The artist himself may help us toward such recognition, as when Tennessee Williams abandons the naturalistic tradition of the modern theater to introduce the much older tradition of an "aside" to the audience, making it plain that more is being said than the play can say in itself, that truth is being presented on more than a single level.

In the arts our time is distinguished by an intense regard for the image of man. Some critical observers of the cultural scene have called this regard an obsession; not a few have labeled it narcissistic. At all events, contemporary art is clearly fascinated by what is happening to the human image, which is always in large part a self-image, and may be said to devote itself chiefly to the showing forth of what being human means. What aesthetic conservatives like Gilson and Ortega y Gasset scorn as "dehumanization" may actually be interpreted in quite another way. One does not go to such trouble to portray human brokenness, erosion, or malignancy unless one is deeply concerned with true and whole humanity. Thus in contemporary sculpture particularly there is evident a tension which is at times almost unbearable between a sense of dark intro-version and self-enclosure and an equally insistent sense of classical poise and dignity. The tension is reinforced by the sculptor's use of different materials in the same work, as by his juxtaposition of rough contours and detailed modeling.

In other arts as well a similar complexity and preoccupation are expressed. There are the symbols of encroachment, absurdity, isolation, diminution, and despair, as we find them notably in Kafka, Camus, Beckett, or Ionesco; nevertheless these tokens of human misery become *ex opere operato* the negative witness to the paradoxical greatness of man which consists, as Pascal wrote, of knowing that one is miserable. Thus by indirection, but hardly by accident, contemporary art is the celebration of the essentially human. Its theme is man's beleaguered, tragi-comic greatness. Its credo, if art may be said to have one, is an affirmation and a defense of man's inherent though sadly corrupted worth. And its purpose, shared and voiced by many in the arts, is that of making visible to man what is happening to him in the refracted light of what he ought to be.

Now it is true that we who are "lovers of art" fail to find satisfaction in this grudging kind of celebration, which comes in by the back door and very seldom announces its presence in a glad and cheerful voice. The psalmist spoke for us all, including the creative artist, when he confessed, "I had fainted, unless I had believed to see the goodness of the Lord in the land of the living." What nourishes the arts, day in, day out, is always the vision of something that is good and needs to be affirmed as such; and by fashioning fresh emblems of that goodness the arts nourish us as well. It is altogether natural that we who are not ourselves artists by vocation should ask for a more positive, uncomplicated affirmation and celebration of life.

But we should be ready to see and appreciate whatever celebration there is in present-day works of art. This means putting aside the stereotypes, the secondhand philistine prejudices—contemporary art is "depressing," "beat," "unintelligible," and so on—in order that we may judge for ourselves. For Christians, and Protestants especially, it means something else. In Philippe Maury's words:

> We are puzzled by art, perhaps because of our inborn puritan tendencies, our conviction that only those pursuits are justifiable which bear immediate and visible fruits. . . . We confuse what is right in God's sight with what we as humans, even as Christians, judge to be spiritually or morally effective. . . . We are concerned that man should do all his work, but we misunderstand the real meaning of God's Sabbath, of God's rest, of the joy of God before his good creation. We have no understanding of the place of esthetic satisfaction before either God's creation or man's achievement in art. . . . We seem to feel that we are permitted to do only those things which are strictly part of our obedience, and not also to enjoy what God has given us through his creation and through the works of our fellow men, to discover in them the beauty of our Creator and the humanity of our fellows.[1]

If Maury's charge is even partly true, then we must sure-

[1] "Faith, Art, and Culture," *The Student World,* No. 2 (1955), pp. 116-17.

ly learn again to enjoy "what God has given," and the stimulus and vehicle of that enjoyment will be exposure to the arts. Delight no less than duty is a proper Christian response to the goodness of creation. And as we turn to the arts with this in mind, we shall be surprised at how much work being done today is truly and profoundly affirmative despite widespread opinion to the contrary.

"The spirit must practice its scales of rejoicing," wrote W. H. Auden in his *Christmas Oratorio*. The image this line evokes in my mind is that of a reluctant child sitting down before the piano to do his finger exercises, making a matter of duty out of what is in truth the rendering of delight. Auden's point, I take it, is that rejoicing does not come easily and therefore must be learned and practiced. St. Paul, you remember, went even further. He commanded his fellow Christians to rejoice—"and again I say, rejoice!"—which most people think is a poor way to begin. If I have to be told to be joyful, constantly reminded of how joyful I ought to be, then where is the joy that is commanded and how am I going to express what I do not already feel without having to be told?

There is a strangely liberating truth in Auden's line, nevertheless. Joy is not necessarily a presently felt emotion; rather, it may be a goal of personal and cultural existence, often imperfectly grasped and sometimes lost sight of altogether, which can still determine the direction of our going and becomes more real as we move more purposefully and patiently toward it. Today this element of promise rather than possession must of necessity predominate, and yet this need not mean that joy is utterly absent or without effect. The human spirit must practice its scales of rejoicing, and in the arts of our time it is doing just that in a most determined and enlivening way.

II

Let us consider further the experience of enjoyment in relation to the Christian faith. If we must be exhorted to rejoice, this is because our faith is lacking in an element that belongs to its fullness, an element which needs to be supplied in order that faith may not languish and die. For it is not as though joy were a reward bestowed upon faith, a kind of satisfaction coming as the result of faith. That would only amount to a hopeless confusion of faith with works; it would withhold the benefit of joy until works-righteousness had earned its credits and gathered in its merits, which makes joy extraneous to the whole enterprise of faith. Moreover, allocating joy to some future state of blessedness consequent upon good performance or obedient action now only serves to poison the springs of lively, authentic faith itself within the present. The Christian faith is simply not itself, it is turned into something else, when the experience of enjoyment is absent from it.

This is not to claim that Christians must somehow manage to be always happy and never sad, nor to deny that the joy of believing may be clouded or withdrawn from us. We do, after all, have to be recalled again and again to the gospel that places us on a new footing before God and our fellow human beings, or we shall sink into what John Bunyan described as the "Slough of Despond." Yet if there is no depth of joy *in* our believing, there can scarcely be joy as the prize of believing. The enjoyment of God is indeed the chief end of man, and this means not his destination alone, but his ever-present purpose and resource. Otherwise the gospel is perverted into the old law from which it sought to free us, and what is intended to be a promise becomes instead a kind of threat which is its very opposite.

Keeping in view this significance of joy both for and within our faith, we may enter more heartily into fruitful dialogue with the arts. For if it is not as though we turned to art to give us an enjoyment which faith cannot give, neither is it as though art had to turn to faith in order to find something to enjoy. There is a common ground for enjoyment in the goodness of creation, a common incentive and occasion for celebration. Art quite as much as faith is a rejoicing in the truth; it may or may not call this truth by the name of God, but that is perhaps a small matter compared to the fact that we may learn to recognize, even in the most godless forms of modern art, God's judgment and mercy as revealed by Christ.

Father Couturier, the Dominican priest who did so much to bring about a changed climate in his own church with reference to the contemporary arts, remarked that while naturally the best thing would be to have geniuses who also were of saintly character, since such men are not easy to find, "it would be safer to turn to geniuses without faith than to believers without talent." Indeed it would, for the reason that it is now the artist who must instruct the believer in the exercise and expression of the capacity for enjoyment that has been so atrophied in Christian circles. It is a matter for thanksgiving that such an opportunity exists today.

It is only the artist, whether he is a believer or not, who has kept alive the vision of the unity of man and nature which a technological and urban culture has made increasingly difficult, if not impossible, for many of us. Superhighways and supermarkets, skyscrapers and satellites, have given us the illusion of separation from and mastery over nature which only the occasional invasion of destructive forces can put in question or remove. But the contemporary artist persists in looking to nature and learning from it; he still turns to nature for a confirmation of his own being as a person and discovers in it echoes and extensions of his manner of life. He seldom exults in nature, like the painters of the Renaissance, nor does he try to copy nature, like his forebears in the nineteenth century; but he looks to the natural world for metaphors by which to body forth what he has found to be true of himself. In this vein Joseph Sittler quotes the lines of Walter de la Mare:

> Very old are the woods;
> And the buds that break
> Out of the *briarèd* boughs,
> When March winds wake,
> So old with their beauty are—
> Oh, no man knows
> Through what wild centuries
> Roves back the rose.[2]

Psychologists may label as "projection" this symbolic self-identification of the artist with his natural environment. Our faith reads things differently, however. Such kinship is primordial; it harks back to the time before

[2] Reprinted by permission of The Literary Trustees of Walter de la Mare and the Society of Authors as their representative.

time was, when the morning stars sang together and all the sons of God shouted for joy. In it there is more than reminiscence of man's innocence before the Fall, which cannot be regained but is never utterly forgotten. Most of all, the unity of man with nature symbolized in art suggests the incarnate lordship of Christ in "all things," as G. K. Chesterton's poem intimates:

> The Christ-child stood at Mary's knee;
> His hair was like a crown,
> And all the flowers looked up at Him,
> And all the stars looked down.[3]

Our common creaturehood before God in the world which God loves—this is a Christian statement of the truth on which all metaphor, image, or melody is premised and made possible. It is the truth to be rejoiced in, celebrated, by both art and faith.

For the most part, this common ground is still a land of promise and not a place of mutual relationship and residence. But there are encouraging signs that this may not be so much longer. Examples of the newer trend come chiefly from architecture and music. One of the best is the Chapel of the Rosary in Vence, France, de-

[3] "A Christmas Carol," from *Collected Poems of G. K. Chesterton*. Reprinted by permission of Miss D. E. Collins and J. M. Dent & Sons, Ltd.

signed wholly by Henri Matisse. When it was completed a Dominican priest exclaimed, "At last we have a gay chapel!" The remark pleased Matisse, who had worked with this goal in mind, creating not only the form and decoration of the building, but also all its furnishings and the vestments used in worship. Jane Dillenberger gives the following description of the chapel:

> The tiny Chapel of the Rosary is alternately bathed in brilliant sunshine and shaded by green-black palms and cypresses. Behind it rise the rocky foothills that join the French Alps, and in front of it the land slopes away toward the Mediterranean. In this grand setting the little chapel nestles serenely on the shoulder of its rocky hill—its flanks gleaming white, its roof as blue as the Mediterranean, and its bell tower rising, as gay as laughter, from the horizontal lines and rectangular shapes of the roof and nave wall.

Speaking of the interior, Mrs. Dillenberger continues:

> The visitor . . . is drawn irresistibly into a vibrantly lovely room, the chapel, luminous with light and color. It has a white floor, ceiling, and walls, but a white that reflects the intense and singing color of the high narrow windows of stained glass. The tree of life provides the motif for the windows. They have a pattern of leaves, simple in form

and in range of color, but with no two shapes alike. Subtle variations of line and level differentiate one from the other, and within the large areas of blue, green, and yellow glass there is a lively range of hue and intensity. These variations give vibrancy and lifefulness to the design.[4]

There follows an account of the somber, jagged composition of the Way of the Cross painted on the rear wall of the nave, with briefer mention of other murals in the lighter, more flowing style characteristic of Matisse.

The chapel at Vence may not "look like a church"; it may nevertheless be a better manifestation of the Church for just that reason. In commissioning Matisse to design the building as a whole and in detail, the Dominican order entrusted the enterprise to a truly great artist of worldwide renown, admired for his sensuous warmth and languous line in the painting of harem beauties and tropical flowers and fruits. The artist was given free rein to express his unique vision and well-known style. The result is a building which provides a new and greatly needed dimension to contemporary Christian worship and witness. The substance of faith is not lost, but instead of being tamely enshrined it is ex-

[4] *Style and Content in Christian Art* (Nashville: Abingdon, 1965), p. 219.

citingly released in a truly celebrative manner. The Chapel of the Rosary, it is hoped, will come to serve as a model for many other small church buildings in other countries, especially in its structural charm and inviting freshness of design.

Further illustrations might be given of this important new trend, notably the church at Assy, also in France, containing work by a group of front-rank artists; single works might be mentioned, such as Henry Moore's sculpture, "Madonna and Child," commissioned for St. Matthew's Church (Anglican) near London, or Graham Sutherland's thrilling tapestry in the new Coventry Cathedral. Here we have heartening evidence that the churches are turning to the arts for help with the formidable problem of communicating faith, and that in the process the churches themselves are being taught some forgotten aspects and motifs of faith. One thing we are learning is that there can be no genuine proclamation of the Christian gospel which is not also its unstinted celebration.

Turning to the arts of musical composition and performance, we find the first steps being taken toward their ancient harmony with faith at the celebrative level. Organist-composers like Jean Langlais and Flor Peeters have enriched the literature of contemporary church music, and their works are being played more and more frequently. There is a great dearth of strong hymns, although service music generally is much improved over nineteenth-century materials. Larger works of more than usual interest—Stravinsky's "Symphony of Psalms," Bernstein's choral symphony "Jeremiah," Randall Thompson's "The Peaceable Kingdom," for example—continue to appear, although their effect on worship is minimal since they are destined for the concert stage rather than the church.

One of the more intriguing phenomena to be considered is the use of jazz in worship. Its idioms and styles belong emphatically to our own time; they arise out of the urban, technological character of our civilization, yet reflect eariler traditions as well, notably the Negro spiritual and the "blues" song. Jazz as it has developed might not be thought suitable for worship because of its association with commercial entertainment. A closer look, however, reveals that elements of jazz are present in the congregational music typical of revival and evangelistic services where organ and piano together provide accompaniment, adding rhythmic drive and improvisation to the basic pattern of the hymns. Whatever loss of dignity may be involved is compensated for by vigor and excitement.

Within the past decade some experiments have been

made with jazz masses. Not all have been distinguished or successful from either the liturgical or the musical point of view; but their performance, while infrequent, has proved helpful at least in loosening up congregational resistance and in raising the right sort of questions about the bland, trite preferences of the majority of church people where music for worship is concerned. We must not be afraid of newness in such music, even though newness by itself is no guarantee of either aesthetic or spiritual worth. One does, after all, like to see some signs of life in Christian worship. Exuberance and vitality and joyous celebration should be natural to the people of God. Sooner or later the style of jazz will be used and tested in the context of worship, just as there has never been a period in which musical styles employed in the church were not also derived from so-called "secular" experience.

What gives jazz its particular importance and interest in relation to church music is that it is mostly improvised music. Jazzmen create as they perform, or perform as they create, exactly like the troubadours and bards of the Middle Ages. They make music spontaneously, yet with regard for certain principles of composition and performance, such as variation on a theme or alternating passages for solo instrument and ensemble playing. Listening to jazz, one is easily reminded of David dancing like a dervish before the ark, or of Psalm 150, which calls into use for worship all the instruments of the Temple orchestra—trumpets, dulcimers, harps, tambourines, violas, organs, and high-sounding cymbals. How tame and staid is Christian worship of today compared with the praise of God recorded in the Bible! This was brought home quite forcibly a short time ago when Duke Ellington and his orchestra gave a concert in a New York church, assisted by four choirs, soloists, and a dancer performing Ellington's own work, "David Danced Before the Lord With All His Might."

These newer developments in music and architecture and the growing response to them on the part of Christians throughout the world may properly be understood as ventures in recovery of the enjoyment so essential to the expression and nurture of our faith. One can only voice the hope that out of these beginnings will come greater resources for celebrating the goodness of creation, recalling Walt Whitman's words from *Leaves of Grass:*

All music is what awakes from you when you are reminded
  by the instruments,
It is not the violins and the cornets, it is not the oboe nor
  the beating drums, nor the score of the baritone singer

who singing his sweet romanza, nor that of the men's chorus, nor that of the women's chorus,
It is nearer and farther than they.

III

Closely tied to the celebrative function of art is the question of whether art can be redemptive. In asking it we draw near again to the central concern of this book. Writing of the new films, Malcolm Boyd expresses his hope that the realistic and revelatory "art of the Fall" may give way to the "art of redemption." [5] Is this a forlorn, an empty hope? Whether art can be redemptive may seem to touch contemporary art most forcefully, but it is also a question that applies to all art. We are asking it here in the following sense: Can art celebrate what God does for us in Christ in such a way that human life is drawn into the orbit of God's redemptive purpose and process?

Actually the question has two parts. The first concerns the fitness of artistic materials and resources for witnessing to the gospel. The second has to do with the character of the response evoked by works of art which have this witnessing function as their aim. The question on both levels has in view the nature of art as a means of

[5] "The Image of Man: Criterion for a Christian Movie," in *Christian Faith and the Contemporary Arts*, p. 158.

grace in the service of Christian faith. But it is broader and deeper too, since it touches upon the significance of a work of art not only in relation to the conveying and awakening of human faith but also to the power of God that saves and makes whole.

To the first part of the question an affirmative answer should be quite easy to give. The arts have certainly proved themselves capable of witnessing to the redemptive Word of God; there is in principle no obstacle or built-in hindrance to this goal. Whether one thinks of a Bach cantata or Grünewald's "Crucifixion," of Milton or Rouault, the viability of the arts to faithful witness is plainly evident. When the artist is a Christian believer his work will document that fact; his belief will enter into the creative process and become germane to the interpretation of the resulting work. It is not a matter of using art for some ulterior purpose, such as giving personal testimony or getting a message across. Quite simply, the witnessing capability of the arts belongs as much to medium as to motivation; it is not imported or imposed from the outside; it is both a creative factor and an aesthetically significant fact. The existence and persistence of Christian art in this witnessing sense constitute a massive if complex historical phenomenon which cannot be gainsaid.

Yet there are problems. Not all the works of art that

witness to our redemption in Christ are created with that purpose in mind. It seems then that conscious intent is not an indispensable element in witnessing art. The artists cited in the preceding paragraph were all themselves Christians and did not hesitate to say so; but we may think of others who, like Matisse in his Vence chapel, create Christian art without adding personal confession to their work. This is an old problem and it is always coming up again. Whatever one might prefer to think, the fact is that the disclosure and embodiment of the gospel in art are not confined to conscious believers in the gospel. But of course this ought not to be an entirely new idea to those whose faith is nourished by the Bible. Does not God use the wrath of men to praise him, and does he not quite regularly turn to unbelieving kings or armies for the execution of his righteous judgments? Why then may he not reveal "the wonders, wonders of his love" through novels, poems, music, sculpture, irrespective of their conscious origins? The testimony of many supports the view that this is what in fact happens.

Another problem arises in the recognition that witnessing art may be of dubious aesthetic value, yet fulfill its purpose admirably. A distinguished professor of philosophy in England, H. A. Hodges, dates his own conversion from the time he saw in a shopkeeper's window a garish lithograph of Jesus washing the disciples' feet. This "art of redemption" could hardly have been great art, and yet it accomplished its purpose with undoubted effect. It could almost be assumed—if not quite—that a certain roughness or gaucherie is even necessary for a truly witnessing art. At any rate it seems to be the case that expertise is not essential.

Are we then driven to the conclusion that what is witnessed to in this kind of art is crucial, while the method and manner of witness are only incidental? Hardly, since any work of art is a unity and cannot be analyzed into a faith-component alongside some purely artistic ones. Moreover, the connections between style and subject matter are intrinsic, not extrinsic, to the work of art itself. Hence any effort to separate them for purposes of theological analysis or aesthetic judgment will be bound to fail. A given subject like the Crucifixion may be rendered in a great variety of styles—say by Rembrandt, Rouault, Dali, or Richier—without losing its character as an event for faith and yet with manifest adaptability to different kinds of meaning or emphasis. Again, it is not necessary that a personally held faith in the good news of redemption should be fully formed in the artist before he can begin to give expression to his faith. He may proceed in the opposite direction, looking toward the place where others' faith is fixed, not in order to exploit a technique but simply "hoping it might be so," as the agnostic Thomas Hardy said of the Christian message.

An "art of redemption" as the representing or portraying of what God has done for us in Christ is therefore a creative possibility and in some cases an aesthetic achievement. But such art is not confined to works that illustrate or decorate the gospel. To the Christian, in a real though elusive sense all things speak of Christ. However, this is probably too general a comment to be very illuminating. The second part of our question presses for an answer: Can art itself redeem us?

Let us be quite sure what we are asking. In theological strictness the question is probably unallowable, for only God can redeem, not human works, however high and holy. We are saved, if we are saved, by God alone. Not even faith can save us. Although we may speak of being "saved by faith," what we actually mean is "saved by grace through faith," as faith is nothing more or less than man's appropriation of God's grace. We should not ask of art what even faith does not presume to give.

Yet when this important point is granted, the question whether art can be redemptive has not been dismissed. It has only been placed within theological boundaries. What remains of the question may be put in this way: Do the arts contribute significantly to the work of redemption from the human end, so to speak? Do they invite us and enable us to participate in "love's redeeming work"? Do they at the very least confirm our faith that this is a redeemable world? My own belief is that a heartily affirmative answer can and should be given.

A work of art does not "save" anybody as a coercive pressure applied from without. Neither, for that matter, does God himself. Salvation happens in a man, not to him. We are saved by what God does to make us whole and well by the inward energizing of his Spirit. To this end we believe that God directs and shapes all things, including human works of art. This belief may be put in the form of a proposition, but what makes such a proposition true is faith's attentiveness and generosity in responding to the multifarious tokens and pledges of God's saving Presence in our midst. There is a sentence by Paul Claudel carved into the wall of the Museum of Man in Paris: "It depends upon you whether I be tomb or treasure." The function of the arts in heightening awareness of what is to be humanly treasured or cherished can never be stressed enough.

Living as we do A.D. and not B.C., on this side of Christmas and Easter, we have much to endure but also much to enjoy. It is not alone the goodness of creation that we delight in, but the goodness of God shown forth in the face of Christ and irradiated throughout the universe, as Teilhard de Chardin expressed it. Because of Christ we know what time it is, who we are, and what the world is really like. The fashioning of symbols for conveying and sharing our delight in God's world, therefore, is the proper business of the artist in every man. And it is Christian business too, whether such fashioning be of material or moral stuff.

To the man or woman of faith, art is an invitation to rejoice in the truth. It may come through many channels and often by an indirection which can be more powerful than direct statement. A still life by Braque or the exuberant improvising of a jazz piano reverberates more tellingly to redemption than Sallman's "Head of Christ." We do not require familiar scenes or favorite words to be brought into the presence of the Love that will not let us go. The final note of art, just as it is that of faith, is joy. A sad song is still a song, for all its sadness. So Lawrence Durrell writes in the opening pages of *Justine* of the "joyous compromise" the artist makes with all that wounded or defeated him, fulfilling it in the imagination.

Redemption has become for many a musty word, redolent of old-time preachers and beat-up hymnbooks. What, it may be asked, has "man come of age" to do with all this talk of ransom and deliverance? Where in contemporary life is any such release or rescue to be found and celebrated? For an answer we must look to the arts, which point the way of our freedom, show forth our restoration, call us to renew our covenant with truth too long imprisoned in the clichés of religion. Art has the great and glorious office of making new the old and sanctifying the new. If that is not participating in the work of redemption, a Christian can hardly know or say what redemption is.

IV

On every hand we are being told today that ours is a functional, operational age, one from which the notes of festivity and solemnity alike must be absent. The world is "sheer world"; things become things to do; the nouns of the earlier metaphysical and religious ages become the verbs of this profane and pragmatic one. Depth and height are both foreign to our experience, intent as it must be upon manipulating means and organizing data. If such generalizations are even partly true, they leave us with unsettling questions about the place and worth of art in a time like ours. Is it any wonder that artists should feel, and therefore act, like displaced persons in a world they never made? Neither is it astonishing that many who are not themselves artists should turn to the arts for instrumental purposes of relief or decoration or synthetic excitement.

In this milieu it may seem that talk of art as celebration lacks both point and substance. What is there to celebrate? Are not the arts reduced to acts of protest or rebellion against the drift of things? Can they do more than diagnose our disease and demonstrate its gravity? If anything is to be celebrated, it would appear to be the triumph of the Fact, the impersonal anonymity of secular urban life, the virtues of the Organization. The arts, however, have shown a singular unwillingness to do this, but have instead registered the shock of such forces with a kind of fascinated horror.

Yet we have already seen how the faithful rendering of the stuff of contemporary experience carries with it a strange and unexpected victory. To express meaninglessness through art is to discover and declare that all is not meaningless, for there is still the artist and his art to be accounted for. Both in principle and in fact art is an "in spite of," to borrow Tillich's term, closely akin in this respect to Christian faith. The artist's refusal to accept the conventional world because he would lead us into the authentic world is itself a matter for celebration and rejoicing.

And this is not all. Not only does art deserve to be

celebrated but it is itself the celebration of life. We are right in looking to works of art for the enhancement and enjoyment of everyday existence, even when we find only what seem to be temperature readings or gestures of protest. The diagnostic and critical properties of contemporary art, although admittedly important, are often greatly exaggerated. Their prominence should not cause us to forget the fact that art exists in every age, including ours, to bless and not to curse man. It means to satisfy and at the same time to expand his aspirations, ardors, and strivings. We are right to turn to it expecting these humane benefits.

There is far more to art as celebration than merely taking something as it stands and calling it good. The "blue guitar" of Picasso and Wallace Stevens does not "play things exactly as they are"; in being played—that is, in becoming art—things are already changed. Whether they are now better or worse is not in question. What really matters is that they have been seen into, have yielded up part of their secret, and are creatively transformed. Such creative transformation, as Berdyaev insisted, is the credential of all genuine art. Art is the bestowal of significance upon the raw materials of our existence; it is celebration in the sense of making known with praise what being human means.

Also it is worth remembering, as we have stressed more than once in the preceding pages, that the artist's explorations beneath the world's surface are made on our behalf and for our good. In order to share his findings with us he may have to "write a new alphabet and make men learn it, . . . pry open their eyes and make them see, unstop their ears and make them hear." [6] That has always been so because men are disinclined to see and hear, preferring merely to look and listen, and so must have their dormant sensibilities awakened. Hence the chiaroscuro of Rembrandt or the atonality of Stravinsky, which provide aesthetic access to a larger, truer world whose very strangeness serves to beckon and enthrall us. Such creative ventures not only inaugurate new styles in painting or music but also stretch our capacity for response in behalf of greater and more durable enjoyment.

There is a considerable measure of truth concealed in the suspicion widely shared in a predominantly functional culture that art is after all a luxury and not a necessity. A work of art bakes no bread and cuts no ice; a culture which judges worth in terms of use will therefore tend to bring the arts into line with its own dominant interests or, when this fails, will regard them as

[6] Lou H. Silberman, "Religion and the Freedom of the Artist," in *Religion in Life,* Winter, 1965, p. 138.

either superfluous or gratuitous. The truth in this misgiving concerning art is that enjoyment, not utility, is recognized to be the prerogative and benefit of artistic creation. Precisely because the arts resist functionalization, their continued presence and encouragement in our society becomes of paramount importance. They bear vital testimony to the fact that man is made not only for duty but also for delight, that his body and soul both need refreshment, enrichment, and enchantment. In our cultural epoch especially, art must be deemed a *necessary* luxury.

That works of art are to be enjoyed and not used is a truth which bears significantly upon the relationship between art and the Christian faith. The principle, obviously, is more a directive than a dogma; it means not that the churches should never use the arts, but that when they do it should be for the purpose of celebrating their faith. Certainly the keynote here is celebration; the arts of the church have as their *raison d'être* the lifting up of men's hearts in praise of God. They are capable of fulfilling this "function," moreover, only as they are welcomed for the sake of the gifts they bring, and not forced into utilitarian bondage.

Some will regard this as dangerous doctrine, and they are not without some justification. Indeed, there is a long tradition in Christian history emphasizing the subservience of art forms to religious ends. In his most recent volume Etienne Gilson champions this conservative view. Citing St. Thomas Aquinas, he contends that in order for art to be religiously valuable, it must successfully fulfill its traditional ecclesiastical assignments: to teach, to remind, and to stir devotional feeling. This means of course that it must represent a subject matter which is recognizably Christian, unless it is merely decorative and hence "abstract." It also means that the orders of art and faith must be kept quite distinct; too much art is in fact an embarrassment or handicap to faith; as Gilson says of Michelangelo's paintings in the Sistine Chapel, "That demigod stands between us and God." [7]

Turning to church music, Gilson does not hesitate to call the masses of Bach and Beethoven "liturgical monstrosities"; in his view they simply assimilate Christian material to the purposes of art. Mozart does not fare any better, for his so-called religious music does not speak to us of God but only of Mozart. At least that is Gilson's verdict.[8] However, the case of Mozart may be judged differently, as by Karl Barth, whose enthusiasm for that composer's music is well known. It was Barth who said

[7] *The Arts of the Beautiful* (New York: Scribner's, 1965), p. 171.

[8] *Ibid.*, p. 175.

that while he supposed the heavenly angels played Bach in the throne room, he felt very sure that when they were off duty they played Mozart for their own enjoyment.

More is involved here than a difference of opinion or taste. Must music first serve the church in order to serve God? Or, broadening the question, is there to be no place in Christian art for what we have been calling celebration—the luxuriant, exuberant, festive affirmation that the world is good because God loves it? If art is always to be kept in its place and not allowed to have its fling, if all we ask is that it should be decorous and not distracting, then must not our worship suffer greatly?

It is clear that the whole line of thought developed in this book leads in a different direction from that espoused by theological conservatism vis-à-vis the arts. We started by avowing the importance of the arts for Christian faith in devising a breakthrough, showing and bodying-forth the human truth about the world as given to us. Then we spoke about the calling of the artist, daring to liken him in certain respects to such religiously accredited yet disturbing personages as the prophet, priest, and saint. Now we have gone even further, reflecting upon the ministry of the arts to faith as the celebration of the goodness of the Lord in the land of the living. Our premise throughout has been that God is not to be confined to what men please to call religion, but speaks and works through the channels of artistic creativity and aesthetic sensitivity as well and as unmistakably.

What then do we conclude? Just this: The mystery which dwells in the heart of Christian faith is too vast and inexhaustible, too auspicious for the human journey, to be hobbled and crippled any longer in dead forms. The grandeur of God, as Gerard Manley Hopkins declared, is forever breaking out of bounds and paying us unexpected visits. To tell the old, old story cannot be enough. More urgent, in our time of dearth, is the office of singing a new song unto the Lord. And for this purpose men of great or little faith will discover in the arts of contemporary life an indispensable incentive and resource—a garment of praise in exchange for the spirit of heaviness.